HOW TO START A BLOG THAT PEOPLE WILL READ

How to create a website, write about a topic you love, develop a loyal readership, and make six figures doing it.

By Mike Omar

This ebook was brought to you by
http://makemoneyfromhomelionsclub.com.

If you are interested in entrepreneurship, making passive income online, and other ways to make money outside of a standard job, be sure to visit http://makemoneyfromhomelionsclub.com!

In the first video lesson you are taught the entire process of how http://mikeomarphotography.com was made from beginning to end, without the need of any coding knowledge, in under one hour!

With the lessons taught there, you will be able to make yourself a professional website with any kind of look that you want.

There are also lessons on Search Engine Optimization (SEO), social media promotion, making mailing lists, selling ebooks and other digital products, developing passive income online, and more. There are also lessons on how to make money with Google, Amazon, and ClickBank (all passive!).

Note: All of the links within this book can be found easily from my main website:

http://makemoneyfromhomelionsclub.com

I love connecting with my readers and something I like to do is personally help them with their online financial goals.

I'd be happy to help you find success in any way that I can.

Please feel free to send me an email telling me who you are, why you are interested in making money online, what your online income goals are, and how you found out about my online school. You can email me via the "contact" page of the LIONS CLUB website.

You can find all of my ebooks at
http://makemoneyfromhomelionsclub.com/amazon

Mike Omar

My books:

HOW TO MAKE A WEBSITE OR BLOG: with WordPress WITHOUT Coding, on your own domain, all in under 2 hours.
http://makemoneyfromhomelionsclub.com/ebook1

HOW TO MAKE MONEY ONLINE: Learn how to make money from home with my step-by-step plan to build a $5000 per month passive income website portfolio (based on building 10 websites that make at least $500 per month each).
http://makemoneyfromhomelionsclub.com/ebook

HOW TO START A BLOG THAT PEOPLE WILL READ: How to create a website, write about a topic you love, develop a loyal readership, and make six figures doing it.
http://makemoneyfromhomelionsclub.com/ebookblog

All of the following websites were made using the exact same techniques outlined in this book and video lessons. Any of these websites will be within your ability to create once you complete the lessons:

Make Money from Home LIONS CLUB – http://makemoneyfromhomelionsclub.com – My main website.

Mike Omar Photography – http://mikeomarphotography.com – My freelancing website where I used to make websites for clients at $500 each (now it simply serves as an example website).

$1,000 / Month Passive Income Website – http://makemoneyfromhomesamplewebsite.com - This is the structure and layout of a $1,000 / Month Passive Income website monetized with with Google Adsense and Amazon Associates.

Sample Sales Page – http://makemoneyfromhomeinfoproduct.com – A samples sales page template that teaches how to make a website designed to sell a digital product.

How to Become a Ticket Broker – http://howtobecomeaticketbroker.net - A live example of one of my passive income websites that makes money selling a digital product (an ebook).

High Quality Outsourcing – http://highqualityoutsourcing.com - If you are interested in outsourcing the entire SEO backlinking process through my personal team (to get high rankings for your website(s) for specific keywords in Google and other searches), you can learn about that service here.

A few important things to keep in mind while reading through this book:

Throughout the book you will be referred to video lessons. While everything in the book and video lessons is as up to date as possible (I frequently update this book and the video lessons), the

place to check for the most up-to-date information is in the *video descriptions* (on the same page you watch the videos). This can be the video descriptions on the pages of the LIONS CLUB website, or the video description of wherever you are watching the videos. Be sure to read the video descriptions of each video *before* watching the video itself.

Also, in this book you will find a lot of concepts are repeated. I know some readers will find this somewhat annoying, but several of my readers have told me they really like this because it really reinforces the most important concepts to take away from this book. That is why the book is written this way.

And most important of all: don't forget to sign up for my free weekly LIONS CLUB newsletter. Not only will you get great information with advice on how to make money online and how to build an online business, it is also where I send out updates regarding ranking strategies, new traffic generation techniques, important announcements, etc. Please sign up here:

http://makemoneyfromhomelionsclub.com/newsletter

Table of Contents

INTRODUCTION

Blogs have the potential to be unbelievably powerful. Never in the history of mankind has such a valuable, simple, and inexpensive tool existed for exploring topics, sharing ideas, connecting with others, and building businesses.

I never dreamed that blogging would lead to more personal and business opportunities, financial success, and clarity of mind and purpose than anything else in my life…but it has.

Blogging, combined with the power of social media, is one of the most powerful tools for massive exposure that exists today…and it's virtually free.

Let me put it this way: Everyone *needs* to have a blog. The potential upside of having one is just too great to ignore.

Not only will a blog offer you opportunities in all kinds of unexpected and immeasurable ways, the writing will force you to organize your thoughts and analyze topics in ways that wouldn't be possible otherwise.

In other words: The benefits that come from blogging will surprise you…over and over again.

In this book I'm going to teach you how to create a professional blog, as well as how to strategically pick your blog topics and write your blog posts (based on keyword research). I'm also going to teach you how to best monetize your blog, promotional strategies that will drive traffic to your blog, and how to create a growing and loyal readership. I also include links within the book to supporting video lessons for extra clarity.

What's great about what I teach you is not only the income level you will accomplish if you follow through creating your blog, but all that you will learn in the process. The skills you learn in this

book will enable you to build all kinds of online businesses and open the door for all kinds of entrepreneurial projects you may have.

Not only that, you will be able to evaluate business ideas much more intelligently once you've gone through this whole process. This is because you will understand the fundamentals of keyword research & analysis, traffic & lead generation, social & affiliate marketing, monetization & conversion testing, and traffic analysis. These skills will help you immensely in ANY business you ever decide to start (online or not, passive or not).

So why wait? Start your blog today!

After all, the longer you wait to start, the more money that is being left on the table.

Note: In this book I refer to several video lessons that can all be found on my main website http://makemoneyfromhomelionsclub.com **in video form!**

*** However, keep in mind that these video lessons were recorded to teach people how to build generic passive income websites with a goal of making $5,000 per month passively (the business model taught in my other book), not major blogs with a loyal readership like I am teaching in this book (so follow the instructions in this book instead of the instructions in the video lessons when creating your blog!). Even so, the information in the videos is valuable in terms of learning how to think about this business and how the Internet works, so I recommend you watch them all anyway and learn as much as you can. After all, understanding the other business model (generic passive income websites) will help you with this business model (major blogs) because both businesses are built on similar principles (so you may as well learn it all – this will help you succeed in the long run)! I personally run both business models for my personal website portfolio.**

Note: All the best resources for building websites and developing an online passive income are on http://makemoneyfromhomelionsclub.com/resources **so you should go ahead and bookmark that page for future reference!**

AN INTRODUCTION TO MAKING MONEY ONLINE

Learning how to make a website is the first step to making money online, and I cover the basics of how to make a website a little later in this book.

Note: Several lessons in this book (including all lessons on how to make a website) can also be found on http://makemoneyfromhomelionsclub.com **in video form!**

The following four chapters are actually the first four newsletters of my weekly LIONS CLUB newsletter (which I highly recommend you sign up for, since it is 100% free – you can do that on my website). I put them in this book because I think they are a fantastic introduction to how building an online passive income website portfolio is actually accomplished. Enjoy!

What are some of the most common methods for making money online?

Freelancing - The first most basic way to make money online is by freelancing (in other words, getting paid to make websites for other people). It's the way I got started in this whole business. More and more people need websites on a daily basis, yet most people never even look into how to make a website at all. If they did, they would realize that putting up a basic website is a simple process that takes less than an hour total and requires no knowledge of coding at all. The very first lesson I teach on my website is the making of http://mikeomarphotography.com (all my lessons are free video lessons that I recorded and put up online).

If you want to make money online, you need to learn how to make a website, plain and simple. Your first website project may as well be a website advertising your new website-making skills!

If you are interested in freelancing websites, you can find advice on how to do that here: http://mikeomarphotography.com/freelancing-advice/

Blogging – Blogging is one of the most common methods for making money online today, and one of the easiest to get started with.

Blogs have the potential to be unbelievably powerful. Never in the history of mankind has such a valuable, simple, and inexpensive tool existed for exploring topics, sharing ideas, connecting with others, and building businesses.

I never dreamed that blogging would lead to more personal and business opportunities, financial success, and clarity of mind and purpose than anything else in my life…but it has.

Blogging, combined with the power of social media, is one of the most powerful tools for massive exposure that exists today…and it's virtually free.

Let me put it this way: Everyone *needs* to have a blog. The potential upside of having one is just too great to ignore.

Not only will a blog offer you opportunities in all kinds of unexpected and immeasurable ways, the writing will force you to organize your thoughts and analyze topics in ways that wouldn't be possible otherwise.

In other words: The benefits that come from blogging will surprise you…over and over again.

Once your blog has either **a)** consistent search engine traffic or **b)** an established and loyal readership (preferably both!), the potential for making money is huge. I cover the most basic monetization techniques for blogs in this very same newsletter.

Go ahead and make yourself a blog about your favorite hobby or

one that follows your experiences with building an online business - personal blogs that develop a regular readership make A LOT of money.

Remember: every day you don't start your blog, money is being left on the table.

To learn how to start a blog *that people will read* in book form (how to create a website, write about a topic you love, develop a loyal readership, and make six figures doing it), click here:

http://makemoneyfromhomelionsclub.com/ebookblog

Google Adsense - This is the simplest monetization method for a passive income website. Basically, you put the Adsense code on your website, people click on the links, and you get paid for every click. Then you receive a check from Google at the end of the month depending on the number of clicks. Plain and simple (in my next newsletter I will explain the entire process behind how Google Adsense works and why Google is one of the richest and most powerful companies in the world).

This method USUALLY makes you the least amount of money of all passive monetization techniques (although in some cases it is the only viable option). That is why you make your initial monetization technique Adsense (to get a foundation eCPM [eCPM is earnings per 1000 impressions] with which to compare the rest of your results from testing).

Once you understand the process of keyword research and Search Engine Optimization (SEO), I show you how to make this sample passive income website: http://makemoneyfromhomesamplewebsite.com/ , a website that is primarily monetized with Google Adsense.

If you build lots of these types of websites, the amount of money you can make passively is pretty much limitless.

To learn how to build a $5,000 per month passive income website portfolio by building 10 of these websites, completely step-by-step in book form, click here:

http://makemoneyfromhomelionsclub.com/ebook

Amazon Associates, Commission Junction, and Other Affiliate Programs - With these programs, you put an affiliate link on your website (this is a link pointing to another website with your tracking ID on it). Then if someone clicks on that link, whatever they buy from that site, you get a commission on (the tracking cookies vary in length, but it could be anything they buy in the next 24 hours to anything they buy in the next 30 days depending on the program). This method is a little more complicated to make money from, but if you do it right, you can do VERY well. This is because so many people go to whatever website from your affiliate link to buy that one product you recommended, but then they decide to do some extra shopping and buy a whole bunch of stuff. That means you get commission on THE ENTIRE PURCHASE!

This method works best for websites where you recommend and review products OR websites where your search engine traffic is highly targeted (i.e. you rank #1 for "toaster ovens" and your website is a bunch of toaster oven reviews with links to Amazon where they can buy them). It also works on blogs you have where you have a regular readership that trusts your opinion and you recommend specific products (using your affiliate link). Websites that are monetized with affiliate links make a KILLING during Christmas (my Amazon websites will make me more in November, December, and January than they do the rest of the year).

Informational Product Websites - These are websites where you sell your own downloadable product. This could be an ebook, software, a video series, or any other product. Basically if you are an expert in any field that people are looking for information on, you can put together an informational product on it (and use whatever medium works best - for making money online, a video series works best). Then put up a website that tells people why the

product you made has value. You can use something like PayPal to charge for your product and then redirect them to a download page after, so it is pretty much a hands-free operation.

There are several third party credit card processing companies you can use to do this (including PayPal), but I personally like to use ClickBank and this is why: ClickBank allows other people to become an affiliate for you very easily. This means that other people can send traffic to my website, and if that person buys a product, I give them a portion of the profit. I like to participate in this program for all my informational product websites and give affiliates a generous 75% commission. I like to participate in the affiliate program because even though I'm giving up a portion of the profits, those are sales I wouldn't have had otherwise. It's a win-win.

On my website, in the more advanced lessons, I teach you the entire creation of this sample digital product sales page website: http://makemoneyfromhomeinfoproduct.com/ . My very first ebook website that I put up years ago was "How to Become a Ticket Broker": http://howtobecomeaticketbroker.net/ , and it continues to make me passive income to this day.

Membership Websites - Membership sites are probably the most complicated ones to start and become successful with, but if you can gain some momentum, these websites will make you the easiest and most consistent money out of any of them! This is basically a website where each member has to pay a monthly fee to gain access. If you charge $30/month to be a member of your website and you have 100 members, that's a steady $3,000 per month, and depending on the type of site you run, you may not have to do anything but maintenance (and you'd probably want to promote too, for more easy money...I mean members!). Include a forum within the website (not hard to do with a WordPress plugin) and some kind of service that keeps them wanting to stay members, and you're set - your new focus becomes getting more members while maintaining the site. And you can offer an affiliate program

too so current members can send you new members that you wouldn't have gotten otherwise.

Those are some of the most common ways for making money online that don't involve shipping physical products (which are E-commerce Websites - yet ANOTHER method for making money online!). The possibilities for making money online are truly endless.

What is the simplest way to make passive money online?

Everyone knows that there is LOTS of money being made online by people all around the world on a daily basis. Every year the amount of money made online grows exponentially and hasn't showed any sign of slowing down, even during this terrible recession. And even though everyone knows that money is being made online, they don't understand HOW money is being made online.

So how exactly are people making money online?

To understand one method of making money online, let's examine one of the most profitable companies in the world: Google. Google commands the most search engine traffic in the world, and as a result is in a very powerful position. Why?

Well let's pretend that we are Nike. Because we are Nike, we want our website to rank #1 for shoes. If we rank #1 for shoes, we are going to get a lot of traffic for people searching for shoes to our website (roughly 42% of searchers to be exact). If we rank #2, we will only get about 25% of that traffic. At #3, about 10%. After that, the numbers start to get pretty low. You may as well not even exist on the Internet if you are on page #2 of the search results.

The exact search item "shoes" is searched for roughly 1,160,000 times per month. If Nike is at rank #1 in Google and getting 42% of that traffic, that is going to translate into almost 500,000 visitors

to the Nike website that are interested in the word "shoes". That is going to translate into A LOT of sales. If it is sitting in spot #3, that would be a little over 100,000 visitors. Still a lot of sales, but MUCH lower. If they aren't in the top 10, they are missing out on a lot of action, and their company will miss out on a lot of potential sales.

And because Google controls where a website ranks, they are in a position of power. If they decide that Adidas is a more relevant search result for shoes than Nike is, Adidas will make much more money online than Nike does on the Internet. And Google has that power over every industry in the world!

So how does that ranking power translate into money for Google? Well, if you ever search for anything in Google, you may notice that the top two or three results have a slightly differently colored background. This is because those are paid search results (as opposed to the natural results below them, which are referred to as organic results). These top (differently colored) results are paid for by those companies so that their links can rank at the top of Google search engine results. Google is basically a lead generator to lots and lots of companies around the world. And whenever a regular searcher clicks on one of those paid links, the owner of that link pays Google for that click.

With millions of searches every single day, Google pulls in A LOT of money. And it makes sense that companies would pay for links, and this is why: Let's say that you are Nike and you know that 1 out of every 50 people that searches for "shoes" online will buy a pair of shoes if they land on www.nike.com. With this knowledge, you can calculate how much you could spend on a Pay-Per-Click (PPC) campaign with Google and be profitable. If the average pair of shoes makes Nike a $50 profit and each click costs an average of $.50, then out of every 50 clicks you pay for, at least one pair of shoes will sell, and therefore you will make a $25 profit (you paid $25 for 50 leads and made $50 profit off of the sale). In other words, if the leads from Google cost you less than amount of profit

18

from those leads, it makes sense to set up a PPC campaign with Google and get your links on the top of the search results.

And Google just pulls in the money from all the companies out there that are doing this, even if it's just a dollar or two at a time (don't forget how many searches there are per day on Google though).

So how does this translate to regular people like ourselves making money online?

Well Google has a program called Google Adsense which allows website owners to put those same paid links on their own websites. And when someone clicks on one of those links on one of those websites, that company pays Google, and then Google pays the website owner a portion of that money.

Therefore, the first step to making a passive income online is to make a website that generates traffic, and the most basic way to monetize that traffic is with Google Adsense.

This is the foundation of everything I teach on my video lessons blog: how to generate free traffic to your websites and how to monetize that traffic. The simplest monetization method to implement is Google Adsense, but eventually I will teach you other monetization techniques for you to test that can result in much higher eCPM (earnings per thousand impressions).

If I want to make money online, where do I start?

I have been making money off the Internet for several years now and have had many websites fail and many websites succeed (succeed meaning they make money passively, fail meaning they don't do anything). Now that I understand how the system works, I understand one of the biggest factors to building a successful website: doing proper research before even starting the process of building a website!

Many people (myself included, when I was a beginner) go about trying to make money online in the wrong order; they have an idea and then build a website based on this idea and then later on hope it pays off. This can cause many hours of work and frustration for a project that never makes a cent, and will cause a lot people to give up on their dream of making money online forever.

What is the correct sequence of action when starting a website to make money online?

Do your research first! What exactly do I mean by that?

Google provides the data for how many times every word (also known as a "keyword") is searched for around the world on a monthly basis. If you go into Google and search for the "Google Keyword Tool," you will be able to look up any keyword you can think of and see how many times it is searched for on a daily basis.

UPDATE: Google got rid of the Google Keyword Tool and replaced it with the Google Keyword Planner. Luckily, the new tool also provides the information we need!

You can also look up the value of that keyword if it is used in a Pay-Per-Click (PPC) campaign. In other words, you can look up how much advertisers will pay Google every time someone clicks on a link and generates a lead for that company. Certain keywords are worth more money than others. This is because the payoff is much higher for certain industries than others (a click for "health insurance" or "buy car" will be much higher than "hair brush" or "white socks"). This is because someone interested in buying health insurance or a car has the potential to spend A LOT more money than someone who might be interested in purchasing a hair brush or white socks.

So why is this information important to someone who is trying to make money online?

Well, with this information we have some very important metrics related to a keyword: how many searches there are per month for that keyword and what the value of that keyword is as a paid lead (also known as the Cost-Per-Click or CPC). We also know what percentage of traffic a #1 ranking in Google will bring on average: 42%. We also know how much Google pays it's publishers (i.e. the people who place their Google Adsense on their website): 68%. We also know the percentage of people who land on your website that will click on a paid link from Google on average (assuming good Ad placement): 4%.

So what can we do with all these numbers?

We can calculate the minimum amount of money a website can make monthly when it ranks for a specific keyword in Google. I say minimum because Google Adsense is generally the lowest money making method for monetizing a website online. It is also the easiest and that is why it is the introductory method I use, but once you become more experienced in making money online, you will learn other monetization methods that can make you much more money with the same amount of traffic to your websites.

So how do I calculate the amount of money a website can make if it ranks #1 for a specific keyword?

The formula is:

(Number of Searches) * (Cost Per Click) * (.42) * (.68) * (.04)

The .42 is the average percentage of visitors that will land on a website that ranks #1, the .68 is the percentage of earnings that Google will pay its publishers, and the .04 is the average percentage of people who will click on your website when they land on your page. So if for example, you look up the keyword "mountain bikes" and find that it is searched for on average 45,000 times and has an average CPC of $1.00, this would be its monthly potential:

21

$$(45,000) * (1.00) * (.42) * (.68) * (.04) = \$514.08$$

You would earn about $514.08 in passive income if your website ranked #1 in Google for "mountain bikes" and you put Google Adsense on your website. If you were to monetize with something like Amazon Associates, Ebay Affiliate Network, Commission Junction, or something else, your earnings could be much higher than that.

Note: If you want to look up some keyword values in the Google Keyword Tool, be sure to look up the EXACT match keywords and not the BROAD match keywords (this is because we want to use only searches that type in that EXACT keyword, not keywords that includes those words or have some mix of them). Also be sure to use the GLOBAL average monthly searches instead of LOCAL (this is because we can drive traffic from all around the world to our website, not just our country).

So now you know the minimum amount of money you will make when you rank #1 in Google for any keyword by using this formula. To start playing around and doing a little research, check out the Google Keyword Tool: https://adwords.google.com/select/KeywordToolExternal . You can also watch a full free VIDEO lesson of me doing actual keyword research using the Google Keyword Tool: http://makemoneyfromhomelionsclub.com/lesson-2-1-how-to-do-keyword-research-for-free-using-the-google-keyword-tool/ .

UPDATE: I have uploaded a new second video on that page showing how to use the new Google Keyword Planner (Video Lesson 2.4), but be sure to watch BOTH videos entirely!

The next step is to figure out how competitive each keyword is by learning how to judge the current top 10 ranking websites for those keywords in Google's search results. You can do this by checking their PageRank. If you want to accurately figure out if YOU can rank a website for one of those keywords without too much work

(because remember, if it's too much work, it's not worth it - easier keywords can be found), you can watch the free VIDEO lesson of me doing competition analysis for keywords using PageRank: http://makemoneyfromhomelionsclub.com/lions-club-2-2-how-to-do-competition-analysis-for-keywords-using-pagerank/ .

I hope you're starting to get an idea of how regular people ACTUALLY make online...by doing research BEFORE they make the website!

The Structure of a $1,000 per Month Passive Income Website

To understand the proper structuring of a $1,000 per month passive income website, you need to understand how Google ranks their websites.

Anyone who has ever heard of Google has probably heard of their "top-secret" algorithm that they use to sort their search results. Well the truth is that the foundation of that "top-secret" algorithm isn't very much of a secret at all (Want to know how everyone knows? Through Google search haha!).

The heart of Google's entire search engine algorithm is links. The more links a website has pointing to it from other websites, the more powerful and authoritative it is in Google's eyes. That's it...that is what it all boils down to. Sure, there are lots of other factors that make Google's results extra accurate and relevant (and a lot of those are still secret), but the number of backlinks to a website are the factor given the most weight.

So why does Google keep claiming that their search algorithm is much more complex than it actually is? Well, one of the main reasons is that it is in Google's best interest to keep their search engine inner-workings mysterious. For one, it keeps competing search engines from using their algorithms (Google is by far the most used search engine because it consistently gives the most relevant results, and they want to keep it that way). Another main

reason is that Google doesn't want any websites trying to manipulate the system to gain a top ranking (remember from my earlier email how much more a #1 ranking is worth than a #5 or #10 ranking?).

Google is very against people trying to manipulate their rankings...they would rather all rankings be natural without anyone trying to artificially inflate their backlinks (this makes sense because they believe that the best results would be produced by the websites that naturally attract the most links). Unfortunately for Google, backlinks are the best way to judge a website's legitimacy and people who are in the business of making money online know this fact very well!

So you have better idea of how it all works, Google ranks each website by assigning it a number called PageRank. A PageRank can be anywhere between 0 and 10, with 10 being the highest possible rank. Google uses these numbers to give a rough assessment on how authoritative a website is, and generally websites with higher PageRank will rank higher in searches for more keywords.

Every time a website links to another website on the web, that means that the website is essentially giving a positive review of that other website. The more links a website has from different sources, the more authoritative that website becomes. Also, if a website with very high authority gives a link to a website with a much lower authority (i.e. - lower PageRank), that website will immediately gain credibility for having gained a link from an already credible site in Google's eyes. To put it plainly, the more links your website has, the better it will rank in Google (especially if some high PageRank websites have linked to your website).

And although Google cannot stop website owners from artificially inflating their PageRank and backlink profiles to get better rankings in searches, they can certainly make it more difficult or scary to do so. They do this by penalizing websites they suspect are engaging in that practice. This is known as black-hat search engine

optimization (SEO) and Google has automatic triggers within its algorithm that will penalize websites that are caught doing black-hat SEO (essentially, shortcuts to gaining better rankings). A penalty can range from pushing your website to the last page of search results temporarily, to a complete deindexing of your website. A deindexing from Google pretty much means the death of a website, as you will never get any significant amount of organic traffic and all your work will be lost.

The practices I teach are white-hat SEO. These practices are the ones that Google encourages. They will bring you slower earnings and traffic numbers at the beginning, but they will make you the most amount of money over time. Not only that, they will safeguard your portfolio so you will never have to worry about penalties from Google (in fact, you will be rewarded in the long run). And trust me when I say you DO NOT want Google to notice that you have been messing around with black-hat SEO (I have friends who have lost website portfolios that were producing over $20,000/month because Google decided to deindex their portfolio due to shady link building practices...all at once).

Developing a steady-growth and passive income portfolio that will be safe and continue to grow for years and years is what my entire program is founded on, and all my free video lessons are founded on white-hat SEO link building practices (that is why the "get rich in 30 days online" Internet courses never work...they don't last long in Google).

So how does this knowledge relate to making a $1,000 per month passive income website? It's because I am going to show you how to structure a website and link building campaign so that each post ranks #1 for their target keyword. Each keyword chosen must have a potential passive earnings income of at least $50 per month, and the website will have at least 20 posts on it. $50 per month * 20 posts = $1,000.

Want to see how an example of how a white-hat SEO website is structured? Check out a fully Search Engine Optimized sample

website that is designed to make $1,000 in passive income per month here: http://makemoneyfromhomesamplewebsite.com/. A full explanation video lesson of how this website was made (and why it was made this way!) can be found here: http://makemoneyfromhomelionsclub.com/lesson-3-1-how-to-make-a-2000-per-month-passive-income-website-using-onsite-seo-pt-1/. Obviously this lesson is relevant only AFTER you do your keyword research! But once you have, you are ready to make your first passive income website. ;)

The next part of the process is learning how to structure a link building campaign: http://makemoneyfromhomelionsclub.com/lesson-5-1-how-to-structure-a-link-building-campaign/. Remember, only white-hat SEO link building practices are taught for a safer portfolio and more money in the long run!

Also note that this passive income website is $1,000 per month because it is based on only 20 posts total. There's no reason not to make a website with 100 keyword researched posts. And then make 10 more of those websites.

Like so many things in life, making money online is a numbers game. More websites + more posts = more traffic = more money. THAT is the foundation of making money online.

PICKING YOUR TOPIC

So are you ready for a dirty little secret about blogging? Here it is: Topic selection is not nearly as important as many people think. There are countless bloggers earning 6 figures, and they are blogging about all kinds of topics.

Not only that, blogs generally transform in topic and style over time - many successful blogs are radically different now than when they were first started.

This is usually because the author learns and grows over time, the author's writing style changes as he finds and develops his voice, and the blog simply starts to morph into what it eventually becomes in a natural progression.

Even though this is true, there are some things you might want to consider before you start your blog:

1) What do you have knowledge or personal experience in?

This is important because your confidence in a subject matter cannot be faked if you don't know anything about it, and your readers will easily pick up on that. Likewise, if you know what you're talking about, the writing will come easily and naturally.

2) What do you love to talk about and discuss with others?

Let's face it: if you want to make money blogging, you're going to be writing about certain topics a lot. Make sure it is something you already love and don't mind discussing with others on a regular basis (especially because we will be writing blog posts that encourage lots of discussion through comments).

3) What would you like to learn more about?

Even if you start your blog only having *some* knowledge on a

certain topic, after a while, you're going to become an expert. You may as well pick a topic you love learning about.

And once you have a few topics in mind, here are a few more things to think about:

1) Is the topic ever-green? In other words, are there endless things to talk about regarding this topic?

Obviously you want a topic that isn't limited in scope!

2) Is there money to be made in this topic? In other words, are there products or services related to this topic that you can promote or sell on your website?

Topics that have a lot of related products are great because you can review and promote them on your website as an affiliate. This is also true about high priced services topics like law, insurance, etc. (lead generation websites make a lot of money!).

There are also examples of websites about topics WITHOUT related products or services that have led to unexpected opportunities for their creators simply due to the high amount of traffic their blogs have generated (I will go over those a little bit later). No matter what, once your website is getting lots of traffic, there is money to be made – no doubt about it.

3) Are there other blogs making money in this topic already?

Do a little bit of research and find out if there are already other blogs making money in the topic(s) you are considering. If there are, that is GOOD news! That means your topic is a definite winner, and you can even study the other websites to see how they are making money. Trust me when I say there is enough money being made on the Internet for EVERYONE, so no concerns about the competition. The overall amount of time being spent on the Internet is only growing every year.

4) Will your topic be relevant 10 years from now?

Think long-term. You want your website to make you growing income for the rest of your life, so I would recommend going for a broad and timeless topic, and not a specific fad (i.e. make a blog about fashion instead of a blog about bell-bottom jeans!).

These are great things to consider, but the most important thing is to simply get your blog up and start writing – doing that will teach you subtleties about blogging than that nothing else can (that is why I am always pushing people to just START!). Experience is always the best teacher.

The only reason I am even mentioning "topic selection" now is because you are going to be buying your domain name soon, and you might want to make it related to the topic you intend to be writing about (although it is certainly not necessary).

I would suggest going for a brandable domain that is somewhat generic in nature, and only putting the topic in your domain if you are absolutely certain that that is what you want your blog to be about.

You can also simply buy a domain like www.YourName.com , without a specific topic in mind, and let your blog surprise you with the direction it takes. If (for example) at some point over the course of your blogging you realize that you love to write about photography and that is what your readers are most responsive to, you can always title your blog "Your Name: My Musings on Photography" and eventually brand your blog as an authority on photography topics.

Other blogs simply write about a variety of topics and the readership is loyal because they like the writer's style and voice – that's perfectly ok too.

A couple of examples that come to mind are Tim Ferriss's http://www.fourhourworkweek.com/blog/ and Maddox's

http://maddox.xmission.com/ (although there are countless examples of successful blogs that don't have a specific topic).

Tim Ferris has a blog that spans a very wide range of topics, yet his following is huge and every single one of this blog posts has a tremendous amount of comments and shares. He has stated (contrary to popular belief) that his blog has helped his book sales much more than his book sales have helped his blog growth. And his books have been on the top of the New York Times best seller list for years. How is that for the power of blogging?

Maddox has a blog that is a collection of critical rants about things he doesn't like. The website didn't make any money for years, except for an online store selling t-shirts related to his website, and that only made him enough to "stay above water." However, his massive readership ended up leading to a book deal, and his first book became a New York Times best seller. He now has two published books!

This is what I mean when I say that topic selection is not critical to success and that blogging can lead to unexpected opportunities.

Later on I will talk about how to pick specific topics to write about for your posts using keyword research to drive the most traffic, but for now, simply get your blog (or blogs) set up.

Note: If you want to buy several domains and start several blogs about different topics, that is a great way to learn, as well as improve your chances of success. Most successful bloggers run several blogs, and many times their most successful ones are not the ones they expected.

HOW TO MAKE A BLOG OR WEBSITE

If you are serious about making money online, the first thing you need to learn is how to make a website - if you don't learn to do this, you'll never be able to make any significant amount of money online, ever.

Today I'm going to show you how to make a website (or blog) on its own domain, without coding, using WordPress (it's a surprisingly simple process). These are professional websites with any look that you want (and can incorporate anything that you want, including social media buttons, "buy now" buttons, mailing list forms, Google maps, etc.).

Note: When I say we will be creating a website using WordPress, I don't mean creating one through the WordPress website. Websites created through there are severely limited in what you can do with them and offer very little flexibility overall. The method I teach enables you to create truly professional websites by installing the WordPress software and you won't be limited in any way.

Not only is WordPress very easy to use, it is 100% free and makes your website completely customizable. Over 15% of websites online have been created with WordPress; if you can use Microsoft Word, you can make a website using WordPress (my LIONS CLUB website (http://makemoneyfromhomelionsclub.com) was made using WordPress...and I don't even know any code!).

Set aside one hour and make your first website TODAY!

The point of today's exercise is simply for you to get your feet wet and to get a website online that you can play and experiment with. Don't worry too much about what this first website is going to be about; just get *something online*. After you complete this first project and feel comfortable with the process of putting together a professional looking website, *then* you can start developing your passive income website portfolio.

If you don't know what to make your first website about, a fun first project could be building a website for your new side business: freelancing websites for others. After all, once you're done with the first four lessons, you'll be qualified to build fairly basic, but professional looking websites. Then you can start charging people $500 per website to make yourself some extra money! When I first learned how to make a website with WordPress, I used to post my services on Craigslist daily, and I would get at least two to three gigs per month. You can simply make your website YourName.com or YourNameWebsiteCreationServices.com. If you decide to go this route, here is some freelancing advice to help you get started: http://mikeomarphotography.com/freelancing-advice

You can also make yourself a blog about your favorite hobby or one that follows your experiences with building an online business - personal blogs that develop a regular readership make A LOT of money.
Remember: Everyday you don't start, money is being left on the table.

You want to make sure you take action as you read through my book or you will find yourself a month down the road without having accomplished anything! If you do have any trouble with building your first website today, simply email me and I will be happy to respond to your email.

In other words, once you have gone through this ebook entirely, you will be a qualified freelance web designer, since most websites will be within your ability to design!

I charge $500 per website to clients, which:

**is MUCH cheaper than my competitors
means I make about $250 per hour!**

What should the domain name of your first website be?

http://YourNameWebsiteDesignServices.com (or something along those lines).

OR http://YourNameLearnsToMakeMoneyOnline.com (or something along those lines).

Want to know what mine is? http://mikeomarphotography.com :)

Note: The following 4 chapters are the first 4 chapters of my other ebook "How to Make a Website or Blog with WordPress WITHOUT Coding, all in under 2 hours!" If you would like to purchase that ebook to get access to ALL the lessons on WordPress, you can purchase it here: http://makemoneyfromhomelionsclub.com/ebook1

Note: Everything you need to build a professional blog or website can be found right in this ebook and on my video series at http://makemoneyfromhomelionsclub.com **. I only mention the ebook for those of you who want *extra* WordPress training.**

Note: ALL the lessons in this ebook can also be found on http://makemoneyfromhomelionsclub.com **in video form!**

The following lessons on how buy a domain, buy a hosting account, connect the two accounts, and install WordPress can also be found in video form on this page: http://makemoneyfromhomelionsclub.com/lesson-1-1-how-to-make-a-website-or-blog-without-coding-using-wordpress/

I suggest you watch that video in addition to the reading below.

How to Buy a Domain(s) and Hosting

The following lessons on how buy a domain, buy a hosting account, connect the two accounts, and install WordPress can also be found in video form on this page: http://makemoneyfromhomelionsclub.com/lesson-1-1-how-to-make-a-website-or-blog-without-coding-using-wordpress/

I suggest you watch that video in addition to the reading below.

There are two things you need to buy in order to own and operate a live website: the domain and the hosting. The domain of the website is the URL or the website address (i.e. http://www.example.com). A standard domain will cost you about $15 / year.

The hosting is where all the information and content of your website is stored. This information is stored on a server somewhere (a server is basically a giant computer) and you pay to rent out some of the space. A standard hosting package will cost you about $10 - $20 / month. Those are the bare essential costs associated with owning and operating a live portfolio of websites (and therefore, an online business).

A good place to buy both of these products is Black Steel Hosting. They offer any available domain names and high quality hosting at a good price and offer 24 / 7 tech support (which is really nice to have whenever things go wrong and you aren't a technical person, like me!).

To start the process of registering a domain and hosting, first click here: http://makemoneyfromhomelionsclub.com/blacksteelhosting

You can also find a link to their website under my resources page here:

http://makemoneyfromhomelionsclub.com/resources

Just go to "Domain Registration and Hosting" and you will see a link to Black Steel Hosting there.

By the way, all my resources for building websites and developing an online passive income are on that page, so you should go ahead and bookmark it for future reference!

After clicking on the link, you will redirected to the Black Steel Hosting homepage. In the center of the screen there will be a blank box where you can type in any domain you are looking for. If you want to go ahead with the project of making yourself a website advertising your new business (freelance web design), go ahead and type in something like http://YourNameWebsites.com or http://YourNameWebsiteCreationServices.com, or something along those lines.

Note: Don't just read along without doing anything; actually build yourself a website now, even if it's just a practice one for fun!

Once you have typed in the domain you want, press the big green button "Search." If the name is available, at the next screen you will see it written in green; if it isn't, you will see it written in red. You can also get the same domain with other endings if you want (.net, .org, .biz, etc.).

Note: If you are interested in developing a brand for your domain, it might be a good idea to buy the .net and .org as well as the .com, even if you don't build anything on those domains (this is simply so nobody else can build a website there). You can just check off all the ones that you want and click on the drop down on the right to specify how long you would like to register each domain for. Once you are finished adding all the domains you want to your cart, press "Order now" to get to the next screen.

Note: If you are going to buy more domains, you'll have to get to the end of the checkout process to the "Order Summary" page, then press the "Continue Shopping" button instead of the "Checkout" button. There you can click on the "Register Domain" link to order more domains before checking out.

On the next screen "Domains Configuration", you have the option to add "ID Protection" to your domains. The way the Internet is set up, by default all websites publicly list the information of the owner (name, address, phone number, etc.). The only way to block this information from being publicly available is to add the "ID

Protection." This will keep the owner's personal information anonymous and block people from being able to find it. Whether you get "ID Protection" for your websites or not is a personal preference, but I like to buy it for my websites.

The "Nameservers" below can be left as is and then press "Update Cart."

The next page is the checkout page, but we've only bought the domain(s) so far, so now we need to buy the hosting. Go ahead and click "Continue Shopping."

At the next screen you'll be taken directly to the "Web Hosting" link. Here you are going to pick between three levels of hosting (depending on your needs). The smallest package is for a single website, so if you know for a fact that you are building only one website, go for that one. The middle package can host up to 10 websites, and for most people reading this, that will be the appropriate package to get. If you are going to be building more than 10 websites, go for the largest package.

Once you select the hosting plan you want, click on "Order Now." On the next screen at "Product Configuration" click on the option "Use a domain already in my shopping cart" and then pick any of the domains you are buying from the drop down menu. The domain you pick will be the main one associated with your hosting account (although it doesn't matter which one you pick...just pick one). Then press "Click to Continue."

On the next screen you'll be at the "Product Configuration" page and can pick your billing cycle. The way the payment plans are set up, the longer you buy in advance, the cheaper the monthly price, so I'd go for at least a year.

Below that, you have the option of adding on the "Backup Restores Program" or "Professional Script Installation." The backups might be a good idea if you are not very tech savvy and would like to be able to have Black Steel Hosting back up your website to any

previously saved backups (in case you mess something up). You also have the "Professional Script Installation" option available if you would like Black Steel Hosting to install WordPress on your domain(s) for you. If you opt for that option, you can skip the "Installing WordPress" chapter. :)

Once you are done, go ahead and press "Add to Cart" and continue on until you get to the final checkout page.

Before pressing "Checkout", some of you may need to get an SSL Certificate. SSL Certificates are for people who need to protect sensitive information that customers will be submitting through your website. Examples include any kind of website where people are submitting personal or credit card information to buy a product, or any kind of website where people are entering login details (membership websites / forums), or any kind of e-commerce website. For any websites like that, you'll need an SSL Certificate (to protect your customer's information).

If you don't need an SSL Certificate for any of your websites, go ahead and press the "Checkout" button and complete your order. If you do need an SSL certificate for any of your websites, click on the "Continue Shopping" button and then click on the "SSL Certificates" link.

Here you will find different levels of SSL Certificates available and can read the descriptions to figure out which one most suits your needs. Once you have picked the one you need, press the "Order Now" button and select the domain you want it for. Then proceed to the checkout page.

At the checkout page you can review your order and make sure everything looks good. If you need additional domains or want to add anything, just click on the "Continue Shopping" button. If you are all set, click on the "Checkout" button and pay for your products.

Note: Write down the password you create during the checkout

process, as you will need it soon!

Once you've finished checking out, you'll get to a confirmation page, and you're all set!

Installing WordPress

The next step is to install WordPress on your domain(s.). First go back to the Black Steel Hosting website and click on the "Client Area" tab. Go ahead and login with your email address and the password you created during the checkout process.

From this area you'll be able to access the products you already own, buy more domains / addons, upgrade hosting, and open support tickets if you need technical support. This is your main "homebase" area where you will start to build your online business from. :)

Once you are logged in, go to the "My Products and Services" page (under "Services", then "My Services"). Your hosting account should be listed there, and then press the "View Details" button of your hosting account. Once you do that, click on the "Login to cPanel" button and a new page will open up.

Note: If your browser says "not safe, do not proceed" or something like that, just ignore it and continue to your cPanel.

Once you are at the cPanel, you're going to scroll down and click on the button that says "WordPress" under the "Softaculous Apps Installer" category. Then press "Install."

These are the options you should pick when installing WordPress:

Choose Protocol: http:// (or if you got SSL, then pick https://).

Choose Domain: Pick the domain you want to install WordPress on. At first, there will only be the domain that your hosting account is associated with. After installing this first one, I'll show you how

to install WordPress on your other domains.

In Directory: Make it blank.

Database Name: Leave as is.

Table Prefix: Leave as is.

Site Name: Pick the name of your website (can be changed later).

Site Description: Pick a tagline for your website (can be changed later or left blank).

Enable Multisite (WPMU): Unchecked.

Admin Username: Pick something (but don't leave it as "admin"!).

Admin Password: Pick something (make it hard!) and write it down somewhere.

Admin Email: Your personal email is fine (can be changed later).

Select Language: This is your preference.

Limit Login Attempts: I would recommend checking this. This installs a plugin that helps prevent brute attacks of people trying to figure out your username and password by temporarily blocking people who have messed up the login information three times in a row.

Under the "Advanced Options" area (these can be chosen based on personal preference, but I wrote down my preferences below):

Disable Update Notifications: Unchecked.

Auto Upgrade: Checked.

Auto Upgrade WordPress Plugins: Unchecked.

Auto Upgrade WordPress Themes: Unchecked.

Automated Backups: Once a week.

Backup Rotation: 4

Then press the "Install" button.

WordPress should now be installed on your website! If you type in your domain into your web browser, you should see a plain looking website without any actual information on it except for your website title and a "Hello world!" announcement in the middle; that is the default WordPress installation.

If you are NOT seeing the default WordPress installation, there are a couple of things you can try first before contacting technical support:

1. Clear the cache on your browser and then reload your website. If you don't know how to do this, just search how in Google with whatever browser you're using (for example search for: how to clear cache on browser Google Chrome or how to clear cache on browser Internet Explorer). It should only take a few minutes to clear your cache. Once you do this, try reloading your website to see if you now have the default WordPress installation on there.

2. Wait some time. Sometimes it takes a while for the whole process to complete with the new domain connecting to the servers and then the installation process. It supposedly can take up to 24 hours for all of this to complete, but I've never seen it take longer than a couple of hours.

Note: To add WordPress to other domains within your account, you have to do one additional step. Within your cPanel, go to "Addon Domains" under the "Domains" category. Once inside, type your domain in the "New Domain Name" box (you must have already purchased this domain earlier and it must be within your

Black Steel Hosting account).

In the "Subdomain or FTP Username" box, pick a username and write it down somewhere.

In the "Document Root" box, the information should have auto-filled in after you typed in your "New Domain Name", so just leave it as is. Then pick your password (make it hard!) and also write it down somewhere. Then press the "Add Domain" button and you are set.

Now start the exact same process as earlier, by scrolling down to the "WordPress" button under the "Softaculous Apps Installer" category. :)

Note: These past 4 chapters are the first 4 chapters of my other book "How to Make a Website or Blog with WordPress WITHOUT Coding, all in under 2 hours!" If you would like to purchase that book to get access to ALL the lessons, you can purchase it here: http://makemoneyfromhomelionsclub.com/ebook1

All the remaining lessons on how to make a website can also be found for free at http://makemoneyfromhomelionsclub.com **in video form (lessons 1.2 - 1.4)!**

Watch these lessons (and make yourself a website) before continuing, as we will be utilizing what you learn to complete your blog in the rest of the book! It should not take you longer than an hour or two to get your first website up. In addition to that, the WordPress platform is very intuitive, so you'll learn how to use it quickly and easily with trial and error.

Note: In these video lessons you will learn how to install free themes for your blog(s). However, if you are trying to create a *professional* **looking blog that attracts a vast and loyal readership (which you should be!), I would recommend looking into using premium themes designed by professional web**

designers (all my major websites use premium themes). They aren't expensive, are highly customizable in ways that free themes usually aren't, and will greatly increase the credibility of your blog.

The best resources for affordable premium WordPress themes can be found on the following page under "Premium Themes":

http://makemoneyfromhomelionsclub.com/resources

Again: all my resources for building websites and developing an online passive income are on that page, so you should go ahead and bookmark it for future reference!

SETTING UP YOUR BLOG AND WRITING YOUR BLOG POSTS

At this point you should have WordPress installed on your domain(s) with the themes that you like best! All that is left is the content!

Before we get to the actual posts you're going to be writing, let's get some of the other (boring) stuff out of the way. We're going to get the pages set up that will add to the credibility of your website and protect you legally.

Pages You Must Add for Legal Protection

For these types of websites or blogs of any kind, there are certain pages you either **should** or **must** add to stay within the terms of service of certain revenue sharing programs (ones that you'll be participating in to generate income). It is also in your best interest to make your website as legitimate as possible, as this will help with the growth process of your website, and adding these pages will help do that.

Note: All pages described can be found on my sample passive income website: http://makemoneyfromhomesamplewebsite.com/

1. Contact – A "Contact" page can be made easily by using the "Contact Form 7" plugin. With this plugin, people can contact you without you having to reveal your email address directly on your website (the installation process is shown in the video lessons mentioned earlier). Encourage people to contact you and connect with you, as this will help your blogging efforts in the long run.

Note: The video lesson with me installing a contact form can be found on the following page:

http://makemoneyfromhomelionsclub.com/lesson-1-3-how-to-add-social-media-buttons-a-contact-form-google-maps-and-paypal-buttons/

2. About – Make an "About" page for your blog, explaining who you are, and the purpose of your blog (don't write to make money!). This is a great chance to introduce yourself to your reading public, so make it as friendly, as personal, and as detailed as you can. Encourage people to interact with you and comment / share your blog posts.

3. Privacy Policy – You are required to have a "Privacy Policy" page with the following information if you use Google Adsense or Amazon Associates to monetize your website (which are methods I teach in this book!). Just copy the information below (also available on the sample website) and you'll be good to go. Don't forget to replace www.YOURWEBSITE.com with YOUR website URL!

Note: The privacy policy below is up to date as of writing this book, but you may want to check for an updated version when you make your websites (just use Google).

*****BEGINNING OF PRIVACY POLICY*****

Privacy Policy for www.YOURWEBSITE.com

If you require any more information or have any questions about our privacy policy, please feel free to contact us by using our contact page.

At www.YOURWEBSITE.com, the privacy of our visitors is of extreme importance to us. This privacy policy document outlines the types of personal information is received and collected by www.YOURWEBSITE.com and how it is used.

Log Files

Like many other Web sites, www.YOURWEBSITE.com makes use of log files. The information inside the log files includes internet protocol (IP) addresses, type of browser, Internet Service Provider (ISP), date/time stamp, referring/exit pages, and number of clicks to analyze trends, administer the site, track user's movement around the site, and gather demographic information. IP addresses, and other such information are not linked to any information that is personally identifiable.

Cookies and Web Beacons

www.YOURWEBSITE.com does not use cookies.

DoubleClick DART Cookie

.:: Google, as a third party vendor, uses cookies to serve ads on www.YOURWEBSITE.com.
.:: Google's use of the DART cookie enables it to serve ads to users based on their visit to www.YOURWEBSITE.com and other sites on the Internet.

.:: Users may opt out of the use of the DART cookie by visiting the Google ad and content network privacy policy at the following URL – http://www.google.com/privacy_ads.html

Some of our advertising partners may use cookies and web beacons on our site. Our advertising partners include ….

Google Adsense
Amazon Associates

These third-party ad servers or ad networks use technology to the advertisements and links that appear on www.YOURWEBSITE.com send directly to your browsers. They automatically receive your IP address when this occurs. Other technologies (such as cookies, JavaScript, or Web Beacons) may also be used by the third-party ad networks to measure the

effectiveness of their advertisements and / or to personalize the advertising content that you see.

www.YOURWEBSITE.com has no access to or control over these cookies that are used by third-party advertisers.

You should consult the respective privacy policies of these third-party ad servers for more detailed information on their practices as well as for instructions about how to opt-out of certain practices. www.YOURWEBSITE.com's privacy policy does not apply to, and we cannot control the activities of, such other advertisers or web sites.

If you wish to disable cookies, you may do so through your individual browser options. More detailed information about cookie management with specific web browsers can be found at the browsers' respective websites.

*****END OF PRIVACY POLICY*****

4. Terms & Conditions – Make a "Terms & Conditions" page to help protect you in case someone tries to sue you because of something they read on your website. While this is very unlikely, it doesn't hurt to have one up. The following one is a generic one that you can use (and of course, don't forget to replace www.YOURWEBSITE.com with YOUR website URL!).

*****BEGINNING OF TERMS & CONDITIONS*****

Terms & Conditions for www.YOURWEBSITE.com

We will always attempt to provide the best and most accurate information possible here at www.YOURWEBSITE.com, but you are responsible for your own actions. We will not be held liable for anything that happens from the use of the information here.

*****END OF TERMS & CONDITIONS*****

Finding Post Topic Ideas Using the Google Keyword Tool

For this chapter, you can watch me doing the keyword research I describe below in a video on this page: http://makemoneyfromhomelionsclub.com/lesson-2-1-how-to-do-keyword-research-for-free-using-the-google-keyword-tool/ .

UPDATE: Google got rid of the Google Keyword Tool and replaced it with the Google Keyword Planner. Luckily, the new tool also provides the information we need! I have uploaded a new second video on that page showing how to use the new Google Keyword Planner (Video Lesson 2.4), but be sure to watch BOTH videos entirely! All the same lessons and concepts still apply.

* However, keep in mind that these video lessons were recorded to teach people how to make generic passive income websites with a goal of making $5,000 per month passively (the model taught in my other book), not major blogs with a loyal readership like I am teaching in this book (so follow the instructions in this book instead of the instructions in the video lessons when creating your blog!). Even so, the information in the videos is valuable in terms of learning how to think about this business and how the Internet works, so I recommend you watch them all anyway and learn as much as you can. After all, understanding the other business model (generic passive income websites) will help you with this business model (major blogs) because both businesses are built on similar principles (so you may as well learn it all – this will help you succeed in the long run)! I personally run both business models for my personal website portfolio.

In this specific video I show additional information to determine the value of keywords that rank #1 in Google search results using a keyword formula. For our purposes, you can simply ignore that and focus on the global monthly searches.

So you've got your blog all set up and you're ready to write your first blog post! What should you write about?

The best way to set up your blog is two have two types of blog posts: some post topics will simply be "free writing" (where you just write about a topic you'd like to write about to your heart's content) and the other post topics will be based on keyword research using the Google Keyword Tool (a much more strategic way of writing blog posts). This combination will be powerful because it will be appealing to readers of your blog AND to the search engines that will send your blog traffic.

The Google Keyword Tool can be used to find the total global monthly searches of any keyword:
https://adwords.google.com/select/keywordtoolexternal

Go ahead and visit that website and start learning how to use the Google Keyword Tool. Start by typing in a random word into the search box. Google will return with a list of related keywords to the initial keyword you typed in, and all those words will have related data columns beside them. The only data column we care about right now is the "global monthly searches" column.

Note: When you go to look up keyword values in the Google Keyword Tool, be sure to look up the EXACT match keywords and not the BROAD match keywords (this is because we want to use only searches that type in that *exact* keyword and no other words mixed in). Also be sure to use the GLOBAL average monthly searches instead of LOCAL (this is because we can drive traffic from all around the world to our website, not just our country).

So now that you have familiarized yourself with the Google Keyword Tool a bit, type in the topic (or one of the topics) you would like to make your blog about. Make sure your setting is on "EXACT".

So for example, if you were to type in the keyword "cement", the results page should look something like this (note that I put the setting on "EXACT"):

So now we have the global monthly search volume of "cement" (60,500 searches in Google), as well as the global monthly searches for a bunch of other related keywords, all listed in the screenshot.

The next step is to download that entire database of keywords as a "CSV for Excel" by pressing the "download" button (the button can be seen on the top left area of the screenshot above).

Now go ahead and do that for all the topics you want your blog to be about or might want to write about. For the example above, say you want to continue with a similar theme to cement: you could make your next Google Keyword Search for "construction" and then download that CSV for Excel. Do this for all the topics you are interested in writing about for your blog, combine all those "CSV for Excel" downloaded keywords into one big Excel sheet, and then list the keywords in order of biggest monthly searches to smallest monthly searches.

This Excel sheet will serve as the place you go to when you are going to write a new post on your blog. Obviously, you generally want to write about the topics with the most monthly searches, but it isn't a bad idea to vary it up and write about interesting keywords that have lower monthly searches as well.

Even though many blog post topics will be chosen strategically based on keyword research, don't forget that some will also be "free written" (this will be explained more in detail later).

This strategy will give you *years* of blog post topics to write about, and you will have a much more clear idea of what people are most interested in within your topic. Writing about topics that interest the most people will help popularize your blog amongst the readers that will comment and share your content, and search engines will also send you more traffic, since your blog posts will be Search Engine Optimized (SEO'd) specifically to appear higher in the rankings for those keywords.

Actually Writing your Blog Posts

So now you have the topic for your blog post and it is time to write! The goal here is to write blog posts that are shared, commented on, or linked to as much as possible. How do we do that?

By making every single post ABSOLUTELY AMAZING! Seems obvious, right? Well it is, but that doesn't mean that it's what most people do. In fact, most people don't write the best pieces they can, even though deep down inside they understand that spending the extra time to make the post the best they can will actually make their lives easier in the long run (if they are trying to popularize their blog, that is).

This is because an amazing blog post will pay you over and over again for years to come. A great post can bring in hundreds or thousands of visitors per day for years and years. It can generate thousands of shares and comments and get your blog linked to from other webmasters that are impressed with your work. Links from other websites will bring in direct traffic from those websites, as well as increase your blog's ranking in the search engine results for several keywords: this is the foundation of Search Engine

Optimization (SEO). This is when you start to see your blog traffic grow exponentially (and as we know, more traffic = more money!).

A mediocre post might bring you some search engine traffic and a handful of shares and comments before the traffic to that post eventually dies forever. And then you'll have to write another post to continue to bring traffic to your blog. So what is truly more work once you consider the benefits…writing a mediocre blog post or writing an incredible one?

Remember, your willingness to not take shortcuts and put in the work is what will make you successful in this business!

Ok, you get it: make your blog posts amazing! But how?

First, make sure your blog post covers a topic thoughtfully and thoroughly. In other words, it deserves to be ranked as the # 1 article in Google for that topic. If you can honestly say an article is as informative as it can be about a certain topic, you've probably written a great article.

Also make sure you speak with complete honesty. Trust is the biggest factor when writing your blog posts. The minute people get a sense that your motive isn't to share or be honest with your readers, you will lose their trust and all your hard work will be lost forever. This is common with bloggers who are constantly promoting products to their public to make affiliate sales and win a commission off their recommendations – their greed takes over as they start to make money by recommending products, and eventually their dishonesty backfires. They lose the people's trust, and as a result lose their readership and lots of potential money in the process. Had they stayed true and only recommended products that were truly valuable, they could have continued to make and grow their income for years.

Trust is hard to develop and easy to lose – stay true to your roots and don't forget why people initially became your readers!

You also want to encourage comments on your blogs and reply to every single one. People like to know that there is a real person behind a blog and also like to be acknowledged when they've commented on a piece. The most successful blogs have a sense of community going on and many people like to comment regularly on a person's blog and participate in full blown discussions. This helps tremendously with SEO because search engines love to see posts that are getting lots of attention - they send traffic to that post because they see that it is popular. Not only that, your blog post is growing in content and getting lots of different opinions on it, making it even more valuable of an article.

In your replies, be courteous and respectful to everyone who writes, even when you disagree with their opinion (this should be obvious, but just thought I'd mention it!).

Note: The writing process can be outsourced and there are lots of bloggers who do it! I personally like to write my own posts, but it is certainly not necessary. If you want to outsource your writing, there are great resources for doing that on my resources page: http://makemoneyfromhomelionsclub.com/resources/ **(under "Content Creation"). The writers there write very well and follow instructions very carefully (you can even send them the instructions and advice in this book if you wish!). You can also order articles on different levels of quality depending on what your needs are.**

Incorporating Basic Search Engine Optimization (SEO) into your Blog Posts

Note: All of the following tips on incorporating SEO into your blog posts are also shown on my video lessons found on the following pages:

http://makemoneyfromhomelionsclub.com/lesson-3-1-how-to-

make-a-2000-per-month-passive-income-website-using-onsite-seo-pt-1/

http://makemoneyfromhomelionsclub.com/lesson-3-2-how-to-make-a-2000-per-month-passive-income-website-using-onsite-seo-pt-2/

http://makemoneyfromhomelionsclub.com/lesson-3-3-how-to-make-a-2000-per-month-passive-income-website-using-onsite-seo-pt-3/

> ⅄ However, keep in mind that these video lessons were recorded to teach people how to make generic passive income websites with a goal of making $5,000 per month passively (the model taught in my other book), not major blogs with a loyal readership like I am teaching in this book (so follow the instructions in this book instead of the instructions in the video lessons when creating your blog!). Even so, the information in the videos is valuable in terms of learning how to think about this business and how the Internet works, so I recommend you watch them all anyway and learn as much as you can. After all, understanding the other business model (generic passive income websites) will help you with this business model (major blogs) because both businesses are built on similar principles (so you may as well learn it all – this will help you succeed in the long run)! I personally run both business models for my personal website portfolio.

Note: If you are interested in outsourcing the entire SEO backlinking process through my personal team, you can learn about that service here: http://highqualityoutsourcing.com/

There are a few easy ways to make your posts more search engine friendly (therefore making them rank higher in search engines).

1. Incorporate the keyword phrase into your title. For example, if

your keyword is "digital camera reviews" make your post title "Top Digital Camera Reviews" (or something similar) and then make a genuine and fantastic post about that.

If two keywords on your list are extremely similar, combine them into the same article (i.e. – if the two keywords are "toaster ovens" and "oven toasters", they should be used in the same article). Primarily target the keyword with the higher search volume, and then you can include the other keyword into the article itself.

Note: If your keyword is "camera reviews digital", do not make your post title awkward by making it something like "Top Camera Reviews Digital" – keep the reader in mind first, not the search engines! In that case, change up the keyword or add some words so that it makes sense, maybe something like "Top Camera Reviews for Digital Models" – this will help you in the long run and won't annoy your human readers.

2. Include four or five related keywords to your main keyword within the article (the way to find these is by typing your main keyword into the Google Keyword Tool, and checking off "Only show ideas closely related to my search terms"). The resulting keywords will be related keywords. For example, the related keywords to "toaster ovens" would be "convection toaster ovens", "black toaster ovens", and "toaster oven reviews." Adding in these additional keywords will drive more traffic to your posts. These related keywords can also help lead the direction of the article and what you should write about.

However, if it doesn't make sense to include these additional related keywords into your article, then don't include them.

3. Include one or two of the OTHER keywords from your main spreadsheet within the article. These keywords will automatically be made into links using a linking plugin we will install later. These links within your articles will help interconnect your website and strengthen the website posts overall.

4. Use categories for your articles. Just make up categories that make sense for your website posts and include each article in the ones that are relevant to make the website easier to navigate (no need to SEO the categories or overthink it!).

5. Add an image or two to each post for added SEO benefit (I showed you how to add images in the introductory videos you watched earlier).

Note: if you don't want to use or take your own photos for your posts, you can purchase royalty free images on websites that sell them for these kinds of purposes. More information and resources on obtaining images can be found at http://makemoneyfromhomelionsclub.com/resources/ **under "Images."**

The first image you upload should have the "title" and "alt text" be the main keyword of the post (obviously the picture should match!). If you choose to upload a second image (and you should!), do the same but for one of the related keywords. These will make your post even more relevant for trying to rank the keyword in Google (and related keywords as well!).

Note: A great trick for obtaining images (and making yourself some extra money in the process!) is by using images from Amazon and linking that image to that page on Amazon with an affiliate link. This way if someone clicks on your image, they are immediately sent to that page on Amazon where they can buy the product. Then anything they buy on the Amazon website for the next 24 hours, you will make a commission off of!

This is a great way to make some extra passive income off of these types of websites, and I use this strategy on ALL of my websites. You can learn more about how to become an Amazon affiliate and set up these kinds of links here: http://makemoneyfromhomelionsclub.com/lesson-4-2-everything-you-need-to-know-about-the-amazon-associates-affiliate-program/

. **Working with Amazon Associates is also covered in greater detail later in the book.**

Writing Non Search Engine Optimized Blog Posts

I just thoroughly described how to make blog posts that are extremely Search Engine Optimized, but we don't want *all* your blog posts to be so strategic – we want a *mix*. Some blog posts should simply be about topics that you are passionate about, regardless of the amount of global monthly searches (if any) that there are. These blog posts could be opinion pieces, observations, random musings, etc. If you have any art blog, your blog post could be "My Favorite Oil Painting and Why" (instead of your keyword targeted posts like "Top 10 Oil Paints Reviews to Buy for your Next Project"). See the difference?

These "free written" posts are the kinds of blog posts that make your blog more human and can really connect you with your readers. Not everyone is comfortable doing this, but the more personal (and even vulnerable) you can be in your writing, the more loyal your audience will become. As your blog grows in readership, more of your posts should be in the "free written" style.

Aside from the benefits of demonstrating that there is a real person behind your blog to grow your following, there is evidence that Google is actively penalizing blogs that are overly Search Engine Optimized. Blogs where every single post is keyword targeted and overstuffed with related keywords have been penalized in search engine rankings. Stay on the safe side and only do partial keyword optimized posts, and leave the rest "free written" (while still keeping in mind all the strategies you have been taught).

If you aren't sure if your blog is balanced enough, consider this: If a regular person were forced to read every single post on your blog, would he ever think some of the posts were redundant? Would he wonder why so many posts seem to have

keywords awkwardly inserted in them, and in some cases delve into topics that don't fit in? If so, your blog is too focused on being Search Engine Optimized, and this will turn off a lot of your readers (and may even get your blog penalized by Google in the search results). Remember to keep your readers in mind first, and the SEO will naturally take care of itself!

A Few More Thoughts Related to Your Blog Posts

How much writing should I do? How long should each article be?

A lot of people ask me these questions wanting a specific answer, but the truth is, it is entirely up to you. There are successful blogs that update several times a day with short and interesting posts that generate lots of interest, just like that are successful blogs that publish nothing but lengthy case studies less than once a month (that also generate lots of interest).

I promise that once you start your blog and start writing, you will get a good idea for how much you want to publish depending on your goals with your blog. I know this answer will sound like it's meaningless, but I promise it isn't: write as many blog posts as you decide is appropriate, and make the blog posts as long as they need to be to sufficiently cover the topic of your post.

In my personal blogs that I've run, I've aimed at writing at least once per week and my blog posts were never less than 500 words long (and some were extensive with several thousands of words and lots of pictures, YouTube videos, etc.). It just depends on the topic. Like I said, there is no right or wrong answer.

A few more tips:

Good "how-to" articles are fantastic. They are incredibly useful and are searched for all the time in Google (remember that most searchers on the Internet are looking for information). A good "how-to" article will be commented on and shared for life – it's the type of article that continues to pay year after year.

Case studies are excellent "link bait" (link bait is the kind of article that generates lots of interest, and as a result is linked to from a lot of websites, bringing your website lots of direct traffic as well as SEO benefits). A long and detailed case study of an experiment performed in the real world will always be popular because people love real life examples of experiments and seeing the results. Imagine an article that was titled "My Exact Diet and Exercise Regime that Resulted in Me Losing 15 lbs. of Fat in One Month, with Pictures and Thoughts." A detailed case study post like that would generate a ton of links, comments, and shares – guaranteed.

For some reason, people love lists, so if you have a good topic you want to write about that could be made into a "top 10 list" or something like that, definitely go for it. What's nice about those article titles is they grab your attention and make you want to read the article. Here are some quick examples of article titles that grab your attention: "6 Easy Ways to Make $100 from Home Today", "Top 3 Proven Daily Exercises to get You Visible Abs in One Month", etc. Of course, even when you make these lists, don't sway from the rule of making every single post of yours AMAZING (i.e. each bullet point should have a full explanation).

At the end of the day, the Google Keyword Tool is *only a guide*, so try to use your common sense when picking your post topics and try and remember that your readers are your ultimate consumers. Respect the trust that they've put in you, and your blog will flourish over time.

Plugins to Install for Top SEO Performance and Configuration Settings

There is only one plugin I absolutely recommend for your blog to help with Search Engine Optimization:

Automatic SEO Links

What the Automatic SEO Links plugin does is it takes any keyword of your choice on your website and turns it into a link pointing to any URL you choose. So for example, if the first entry you added to the plugin was the keyword "blue widget" and the URL "www.YOURWEBSITE.com/blue-widget" , then every time the keyword "blue widget" was somewhere on your website, it would automatically be turned into a link that points to "www.YOURWEBSITE.com/blue-widget" .

This is why I've had you insert one or two OTHER keywords from your list into all of your articles. This plugin turns those keywords into links and helps interconnect the entire website, giving it an added SEO benefit.

Note: How to install and configure this plugin is shown on the video lesson mentioned earlier in this chapter (lesson 3.1).

SEO General Website Settings

Note: I show you the actual configuration of the following settings in my video mentioned earlier in this chapter (lesson 3.2).

This is how you should configure your website settings to ensure top SEO performance. They are all listed under "settings" in the backend.

1. Reading – For this section, make sure the homepage is displaying your latest posts. Pick a number between 5 and 10 posts to display (based on your preference) and set your homepage to display full posts.

2. Privacy – Make sure this is set to "I would like my website to be visible to everyone…"

3. Permalinks – In this one, you want to set the option to "custom setting" for your permalinks and type in exactly this: /%postname%/ . What this will do is set up the URL of each page of your website to match the post title or page title, giving you an extra SEO boost for their targeted keywords.

The rest of the website settings can be modified to your preference, but as far as SEO is concerned, they are fine at their default settings.

How to Setup Your Sidebar and Widgets for Full SEO Benefit

Setting up your sidebar for full SEO benefit is not difficult to do. Simply make sure you have "Recent Posts" and "Categories" in the sidebar. For "Recent Posts", have it display the maximum amount of posts it allows (should be 20). Aside from that, no other widgets are necessary for SEO – all the rest of the widgets can be set up however you prefer – just remember to keep your readers' best interest in mind (as you always should!).

Note: If you are interested in outsourcing the entire SEO backlinking process through my personal team, you can learn about that service here: http://highqualityoutsourcing.com/

MONETIZING YOUR BLOG

Now that you know how to write your posts and do some basic Seach Engine Optimization (SEO), it is time to monetize your website! Remember: there are hundreds of ways to make money off of a website that is generating traffic (and I encourage doing lots of testing and experimenting to squeeze the most money that you possibly can out of each website!). However, don't forget to always respect your readers in the process. If your blog has too many advertisements, is over-promotional, or turns off your readers in some other way, all your hard work will be lost!

For this chapter, you can watch me monetizing a website with Google Adsense and Amazon Associates in the two video lessons on this page: http://makemoneyfromhomelionsclub.com/category/blog/part-4-monetization/ **. I highly suggest watching both of these videos in addition to the reading below.**

Monetizing with Google Adsense

The first technique I am going to show you for monetizing a website is with Google Adsense. This is traditionally the easiest way to monetize a website or blog, and generally the method with the lowest eCPM (earnings per thousand impressions). In spite of it usually being the lowest earning method, it is the easiest to implement, and therefore, the most common method. It is the method I primarily recommend for the other business model I teach (based on generic passive income websites).

While you are just starting off your blog, this method will be fine, but once your blog starts getting regular traffic or a regular readership, I would suggest getting rid of Google Adsense and start testing other monetization techniques that will be more profitable.

Putting Google Adsense on a website is a fairly easy process, especially a WordPress website. The first thing you need to do is

apply for a Google Adsense account by clicking here:
http://www.google.com/adsense/.

Note: To apply for a Google Adsense account, you need to have first built a website.

Creating Google Adsense Units for Your Website

Once you are approved for a Google Adsense account (this could take a few days), you are ready to create ad units for your websites.

To create your first ad unit, first visit http://www.google.com/adsense/ . On this page click on the "My Ads" button and then press "+ New Ad Unit" button.

Here is a screenshot of the page where you will be designing your ad:

For the title box of this ad unit, enter the name of the website you are designing your ad for. Next you will pick the size of your ad (pick either the "160x60 wide skyscraper" or the "336x280 large rectangle". For ad type, select "text ads only" (since those are the ad types that generally have the highest eCPM and will generate the most money).

The rest of the settings can be left at their default, except possibly the color palette, which you may want to modify, so that the ad unit matches your website colors.

Once you are done setting up your ad unit, press the "Save and Get Code" button and copy the HTML code that Google gives you. Paste that code on a document because you are going to need it soon. Now do the exact same process described above for a new ad unit, but this time select the other ad size.

You should finish this process with the HTML code for the "160x60 wide skyscraper" ad unit and the "336x280 large rectangle" ad unit.

Best Google Adsense Unit Sizes and Placements for Your Website

Different webmasters recommend different ad sizes and placements for a website, but the setup I am recommending is good for a few reasons:

1) It produces a good overall click-through-rate ("CTR"). Remember that the more clicks your ads get, the more money you make!

2) The setup isn't overly aggressive or spammy (which is against the Google Adsense Terms of Service and could get you banned from the Google Adsense program). You want a website that is balanced: it clearly has ads on it (that will produce clicks), but not so many ads that the visitor experience is worsened because of them, or that visitors are "tricked" or "forced" into clicking on the ads.

On these websites, I recommend the following ad sizes and placements:

1) In the top of the sidebar will go the "160x60 wide skyscraper" ad unit. Make a text widget titled "Ads by Google", and within the widget you will place the ad unit HTML code (this is done by placing the HTML code Google gave you directly into the widget…it's as simple as that!). This ad block will show up on your sidebar, which means it will show up on every single page of your website. Once you do this, your ad will be live!

2) On each post of your website, there will be two "336x280 large rectangle" ad units. One will be on the top right of your post, and the other directly beneath the post. These ads will show up anytime someone clicks on a post of your website, and they will be visible on the posts that are displayed on the homepage of your website as well. I will show you how to place these later in the chapter, since the process is a little more complex.

These sizes and placements will give you excellent CTR but also keep your Google Adsense account safe because the placement isn't too spammy.

Note: The setup described above is exactly the one shown on my sample website:
http://makemoneyfromhomesamplewebsite.com/

Installing the Google Adsense Units on Your Website

Installing the "160x60 wide skyscraper" ad unit on your sidebar is very easy, but installing the two "336x280 large rectangle" ad units on your posts is a little trickier.

The easiest method for setting up your Google Adsense ad blocks is by installing the "Ozh Who Sees Ads" plugin. Go ahead and install that plugin.

Once it is installed, go to the settings of the plugin (under "settings" of your backend), and you're going to make a new entry. Where it says "new context" and then "Name:", write "bottom post." Then down below where it says "Ad Code:", paste in your

HTML ad code for the "336x280 large rectangle" ad unit. The rest of the settings can be left at their defaults. Save that entry.

Next, we're going to do this process again, but slightly differently. This time next to "Name:", write "top post."

Then next to "Ad Code:", you're going to paste this in exactly:

```
<div style="display:block;float:right;margin: 0px 10px 0px 0px;">
"Adsense code"
</div>
```

Just replace the part that says "Adsense code" with the actual HTML code you have saved (the same one you used earlier). The reason we inserted that extra bit of code is because we want the ad unit to slide to the right of the post, with the text wrapping around it. Save this entry too.

Once this is done, go to any post you have on your website (this process I'm about to describe is something you'll have to repeat for every post on your website). Once you click on the post, make sure you are in the "HTML" view of your entry. On the tool bar, you will see a dropdown button that wasn't there before, and in the dropdown you'll see the two entries you made ("bottom post" and "top post").

At the very beginning of your entry put in "top post" (by pressing "top post" on the dropdown menu button) and at the very end of your entry put in "bottom post" (by pressing "bottom post" on the dropdown menu button). Each time you did this a little bit of code should have been inserted into your post. Now save the post and take a look! Your ad blocks should now be live.

What this plugin does is it will insert that code that you setup in your plugin earlier directly into your post. When you look at your post, you should see the Google Adsense blocks on there.

Now do this for all the posts on your website, and your website will be optimally monetized with Google Adsense ads, but in a subtle and safe way.

Note: Do not ever click on your own ads to make money (or have friends do it, etc.)! If Google suspects that you have been doing this, they will ban you from the Google Adsense program. It simply isn't worth the risk!

Note: Remember that Google Adsense is only a temporary monetization method, and once your blog starts getting regular traffic or a regular readership, get rid of Google Adsense and find some more profitable monetization techniques.

Monetizing with Amazon Associates and Other Affiliates

Another way to monetize your website is with Amazon Associates. The way the Amazon Associates program works is you put your specific Amazon Associates affiliate link anywhere on the Internet, and anytime anyone clicks on that link they are redirected to the Amazon website (to a page of your choice). You will receive a commission on anything that person buys off of Amazon in the next 24 hours (anywhere between 4% and 8%, depending on how many products you've sold that month).

Once you have a regular readership that trusts you, Amazon Associates becomes an incredible monetization technique. You can promote products on your blog posts explaining why you like them and recommend them, link to those products on Amazon, and when people buy them, you make money! This is why trust is such an important factor in making money from your blog (and why you can't abuse that trust once you have it).

For example, if you have a tech blog with a regular readership, you can put up posts like "tech gadget reviews", "my favorite electronics", "top 10 gizmos of the year", "best tech Christmas

presents", etc. all linking to Amazon with your affiliate link. See how this can be such a money maker?

And not only will these posts make money the day you put them up when your regular audience reads them, but they will continue to make money from new blog visitors from search engines who find old blog posts of yours. This is why blogs make more money year after year: because each year your blog grows in content and traffic. And as always in this business, more content = more traffic = more money.

To sign up for the Amazon Associates program, first visit https://affiliate-program.amazon.com/ and register for an account. Once you are registered and logged in, whenever you visit Amazon, you will notice a new gray toolbar along the top of your web browser. With this toolbar, you can get your Amazon Associates affiliate link to any page on Amazon.

For example, type in a product like "toaster ovens" into the search bar and click on one of them. At this product page, you can now click on the "Link to this page" button on the top left, and get your affiliate link HTML code. The link they give you will connect to that toaster oven page with your affiliate information. It's that simple!

On that page, they allow you to get the HTML code for the "image and text", the "text only", and the "image only", as you can see on the following screenshot:

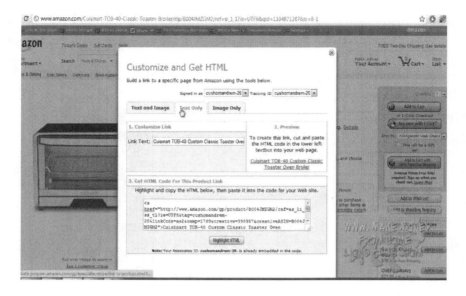

I like to copy out the actual URL instead of the entire code, and then insert it where I need to on my website, but how you set it up is up to you!

So now that you know how to get your affiliate links from Amazon, where on the website should they go? Well, as mentioned earlier, a great way to get images for your website is from Amazon, and then have the images link to Amazon with your specific affiliate link. So for every picture you have on your website, make it link to that specific Amazon page selling that product with your affiliate link. Also include a "call to action" text affiliate link somewhere on that same post for each picture too (i.e. something like "Click here to buy this product!"). This will inevitably generate some affiliate sales off of your post!

Another trick I use to make money from Amazon Associates is adding a simple affiliate text link on the top right of my website in the sidebar. For example, for a blog that is about construction and cement products, the text link would say something like "Click here for the widest selection and bestselling concrete and cement construction products!" and the link would point to the homepage of Amazon (or maybe the main construction section of Amazon).

Then I will make a commission off of anything that visitor buys for the next 24 hours. Simple and effective!

Amazon Associates is one of the top affiliate marketing programs that exists, but it is certainly not the only one. It is my favorite one for physical products though, because they sell just about every product you can think of. Not only that, but people already trust Amazon, so conversion is always good once they land on their page.

There are several affiliate programs that exist and some may fit in with your blog better than Amazon. For example, if you have a blog about self-help and actualization, maybe the best product for you to promote is an informational product instead of a physical one. In that case, I would look for a product to promote on ClickBank, since they specialize on selling information products like ebooks, video courses, etc.

Other top rated affiliate programs include cj.com, shareasale.com, linkshare.com, and e-junkie.com. Unless you have a blog about a really specific niche topic, it's unlikely you'll have to look much further than those affiliate programs to be able to promote the products that you want on your blog.

How to set up a Mailing List / Automated Newsletter and Best Practices

Note: You can watch me set up a mailing list and newsletter on the video lesson on the following page:

http://makemoneyfromhomelionsclub.com/lesson-8-1-how-to-set-up-a-mailing-list-and-autoresponder-newsletter-with-aweber/

*** Don't forget to sign up for the 100% free LIONS CLUB weekly newsletter on my website (it also serves as a live example of what I teach here)!**

No website (or Facebook fan page, etc.) is complete until it has a sign up form to collect email addresses (otherwise, you're leaving money on the table). Every business in the world should have an email list, as well as a newsletter they send out on a regular basis. No matter what kind of online website you have (business website, personal blog, etc.), get a sign up form on there and start collecting emails immediately (even if you don't have a clear idea of what you're going to do with that mailing list yet). One of the most common regrets of anyone with an online presence is "not having started collecting emails sooner."

Here are a few of the advantages to having an emailing list:

- ⋏ Your mailing list will never die, no matter what might happen to your website or business.
- ⋏ The newsletter is a constant reminder of your business / services / etc.
- ⋏ It is a much more personal way of communicating with your audience.
- ⋏ It is the most effective way to communicate with your entire audience at once about time sensitive issues (announcements, special promotions, contests, etc.).

Here are a few important tips you don't want to forget when setting up your emailing list:

- ⋏ Get your mailing list set up as soon as you start your blog and start collecting email addresses as soon as possible.
- ⋏ A great way to get people to subscribe to your newsletter is to promise them something really cool for signing up! This could be a free ebook, a special coupon, or anything else. For mine, I promise that the "thank you" page will make them laugh.
- ⋏ Tell them in the welcome email to "whitelist" your email address so that your newsletter doesn't get blocked by spam filters. Also include in the welcome email what they should expect from your newsletter.
- ⋏ Make sure your sign up form is somewhere prominent on your website: getting each visitor to sign up for your

mailing list should be a top goal.

- ⋏ Employ the same strategy you do with your social networks: every time you publish a new post, take a few extra minutes to send out a newsletter with a link to the post to your subscriber list.
- ⋏ Your newsletter is a great platform to sell and promote products. However, don't sell or promote products in every newsletter you send, or your audience will get annoyed and unsubscribe. Do your selling and promotion sparingly.

Make sure sending useful and informative content is your top priority, and your audience will stay loyal and won't ever want to unsubscribe.

In the video lesson I teach you how to set up a mailing list and autoresponder newsletter. This includes how to do automated messages with preset time intervals, as well as one-time broadcasts. I go over how to set up an inbox sign up form and a lightbox sign up form (the one that pops up). I also go over best practices for setting your mailing list so you grow your list faster and build a loyal following.

To watch the video lesson, click here:

http://makemoneyfromhomelionsclub.com/lesson-8-1-how-to-set-up-a-mailing-list-and-autoresponder-newsletter-with-aweber/

Selling Advertisements

Selling advertisements is another way blogs with a regular readership can make money online. Although there are bloggers who have managed to strike some very lucrative deals with independent companies for advertising space on their blog, I generally find that this is not as lucrative as placing affiliate advertisements in that same space.

Even so, if you are interested in exploring this option, it is not that difficult to do. Contact companies in your same niche that might be

interested in advertising on your website, and let them know that you are selling space on your blog. If they are interested, they'll generally want to know how much traffic your blog is getting, where their advertisement(s) would go, and how much it would cost per month / year / etc. If you find that what they're willing to pay is more than you've been making from putting Google Adsense or affiliate links / banners in that same spot of your blog, then go with the deal.

However, there is one final option you'll want to try before going that route.

How to Create Your Own Digital Product

In my opinion, this is what separates the big boys from most online bloggers. Once you are selling your own product (instead of advertising other people's products), that is when your profit margins skyrocket and you can start to make some real money. Obviously there are people who make TONS of money with only Google Adsense or affiliate marketing (and those are certainly easier methods for making money online than creating your own product), but the biggest profit margins exist once you are selling your own product since you are no longer operating as a middleman. This is why I always recommend selling your own product as the final goal for your blog. I don't suggest you make that product until you have a regular readership (because knowing your audience will really guide the type of product you create), but that should be your eventual goal. Up until then, Google Adsense and affiliate marketing is a good place to start, and then eventually affiliate marketing combined with selling your own product(s), or only selling your own product(s).

Another advantage of a digital product is the fact that it is *digital*. You are essentially selling a computer file. In other words, no production costs, no inventory costs, no shipping costs, or any other headaches. When someone buys your product, the money is deposited directly into your bank account and the customer is

automatically redirected to a download page to receive their product. It is essentially a hands free operation once it is set up.

Plus with your own digital product, you can recruit other affiliate marketers to promote your product for you (paying them a commission for any converted sale). Essentially, you are getting others to do marketing for your blog. This process of recruiting affiliates and paying them out can also be completely automated and is discussed later in this book.

My best advice when creating your digital product is simply to make it the best product that it can be. If you make a fantastic product, everything else will become much easier. It will be easier to sell your product, have satisfied buyers recommend your product to others, and recruit powerful affiliates to promote your product.

Note: Another great reason for interacting with your community of readers on a regular basis is that it is a great way to find out what people would want from an informational product that you create. You can figure out what kind of content they would want you to include in your product and what problems they want solutions for. Not only that, once you release your product, you will already have a pool of potential buyers. And because you've already established a relationship with them, they will usually be willing to recommend your product to others (which is the most powerful kind of promotion you can hope for).

Ebooks

Ebooks are the simplest product to create, so I suggest you start with that. Even though writing an ebook seems like a daunting task, it really isn't. I'll actually tell you how I wrote this ebook (and other ebooks I've written) and you'll see that it's actually fairly simple to do.

Once you are at a point where you are going to write an ebook, you should probably already be an expert on your topic (you've already

been running your blog for a while, had lots of discussions, etc.). So even though you'll have to do some research for certain parts, most of the content will come from personal knowledge and experience.

What I've done to write all my ebooks is start by making an overall outline of everything I want to cover. I pretty much make a Table of Contents before I start writing, and under each section I write bullet points of absolutely everything I want to make sure I cover. From that point on, it isn't that different from writing blog posts, because I write each section once at a time. Every time I sit at my computer I try to complete one section and just work through the whole thing.

Once all the sections are filled out, I reread, do some editing and formatting, reread again to make sure it's perfect, and it's done! Then I get the ebook cover created and it's done!

Note: I do NOT do graphic design at all. To make my ebook covers (or other similar projects), I use www.fiverr.com **. At a lot of points during your time building your blog (and online business), you're going to run into problems. Don't let that stop you from making progress! Find a way to resolve the issue, learn from the experience, and keep moving forward!**

Video Series

Another popular item you can sell is a video or video series. Sometimes a video series is a much easier medium for teaching something than an ebook. This is the case for a lot of the Internet stuff that I teach, which is why I have all these video lessons to go with the ebook.

Recording my videos was actually not that difficult because I used screen capturing software, which meant I would hit the record button, and anything happening on my screen was being recorded, and anything audio in the room was recorded by the computer microphone (so make sure to be working in a quiet place when you

are recording!). Then I hit stop when I finished that segment, and recorded the next segment. Once all the segments were done, I'd put them together and have the software make a video for me (a computer file). Video complete!

Note: For the screen capture software that I've used, visit my resources page and click on "Video Recording Software":

http://makemoneyfromhomelionsclub.com/resources/

Membership Websites, Audio Files, Software, and Other Products

Ebooks and video series are the most common products to create and sell on a blog, but just about any digital product can be sold in a hands free and passive manner. If you produce music or any other type of audio, you can sell it on your blog. If you produce different kinds of software, that can be sold on your blog as well.

A membership website is essentially a continual selling of your products: people pay a monthly fee to be a part of your website and get access to exclusive content (this can include ebooks, videos, software, forum access, etc.). This is an awesome model because as your membership grows, you make more and more money on a monthly basis, but your workload (if any) remains the same.

And those numbers can add up fast! Think about it: if your membership website costs $33 / month, 100 members will make you $3,300 / month. 300 members will make you $9,900 / month. 1000 members will make you $33,000 / month. See what I mean?

Note: For the top membership software, visit my resources page and click on "Membership Websites":

http://makemoneyfromhomelionsclub.com/resources/

How to Sell Your Own Product

Once you have created your product, it is time to sell! I recommend selling your digital products through ClickBank.

Full video tutorials on how to set up and sell your digital products through ClickBank can be found on the following two pages:

http://makemoneyfromhomelionsclub.com/lesson-7-1-how-to-make-a-powerful-sales-page/

http://makemoneyfromhomelionsclub.com/lesson-7-2-how-to-sell-a-product-on-clickbank-payment-page-download-page-and-affiliate-program/

ClickBank is the biggest online marketplace for digital information products that exists. And beyond making the process of selling a digital product extremely easy and secure for you, there is one reason in particular I recommend working with them over anyone else: they have the biggest network of affiliate marketers.

In other words, once you are selling your own product through ClickBank, there is a whole network of affiliate network marketers that can promote your product, and you can choose the amount of commission that you pay them (and the whole process is automated – ClickBank does all the tracking and pays the affiliates for you). This is essentially the same way you can make money promoting products as an affiliate for Amazon and others, except now other people are promoting *your* products. And ClickBank encourages their affiliates to look for products to promote that exist in their marketplace, so just setting up a product with ClickBank could get you some affiliates right away.

Once your product is set up and officially on sale, you can then *actively* recruit affiliates to promote your product, and essentially have them do a bunch of marketing for you. Just reach out to other bloggers in your niche with an email explaining who you are, what

your product is, and how much commission you'll pay them if they promote your product. Most bloggers are aware of affiliate marketing and will immediately know what you're talking about.

I sell my ebook "How to Become a Ticket Broker" on my website http://howtobecomeaticketbroker.net through ClickBank and offer affiliates 75% for any sale made through their affiliate link. I don't mind paying such a high commission, because at the end of the day, those are sales I wouldn't have had otherwise. It's a win-win!

Note: Become an affiliate for my ticket broker ebook, and you will earn 75% off of every single sale made!

Note: To sign up for a ClickBank account, click here:

http://makemoneyfromhomelionsclub.com/clickbank

You can also visit my resources page and click on "Affiliate Programs and Product Distribution":

http://makemoneyfromhomelionsclub.com/resources/

PROMOTING YOUR BLOG

At this point you know how to properly set up your blog, write content for your blog, and monetize it. Now it is time to get some exposure and drive some serious traffic! There are a lot of ways to promote your blog that will not only get you some immediate and direct traffic, but will continue to give you traffic for years due to positive Search Engine Optimization (SEO) benefits as well.

The interesting thing about online traffic is that the combination of social exposure and positive SEO leads to even more social exposure and positive SEO, which is why the traffic to a blog starts slow but grows exponentially with time.

Note: If you are interested in outsourcing the entire SEO backlinking process through my personal team, you can learn about that service here: http://highqualityoutsourcing.com/

Installing Google Analytics for Tracking

Note: You can watch me installing Google Analytics in the second half of my video lesson about Google Adsense found on this page: http://makemoneyfromhomelionsclub.com/lesson-4-1-everything-you-need-to-know-about-google-adsense/ **. I highly suggest watching this video in addition to the reading below.**

Google Analytics is a fantastic piece of software that tracks all the traffic to a website and provides all kinds of interesting statistics regarding that traffic. It is something I install on every website I make right at the beginning of the process, because that information that it collects over time becomes very valuable later on (especially when figuring out the most intelligent way to expand your websites and continue promotion). Not only is this software extremely useful, it is completely free!

To install Google Analytics on your website, the first thing you do is visit http://www.google.com/analytics/ and register for an account. Once you are registered, you are going to click on "Create New Website Profile." Then type in the URL of your website that you'd like to track, and then press "Finish." On the next screen Google will give you the Analytics HTML code. Take that code and paste it onto a document because you are going to need it soon.

Now go back to your website backend and click on "Appearance" and then click on "Editor." We are about to look at the HTML / CSS code on the backend of the website – the code can be a little intimidating but don't be scared! This is how a website backend truly looks like when constructed from scratch (instead of made with WordPress).

Once you are on the editor screen, click on "header.php" on the right hand side. Once you are at this document, search for the line that says "</head>". That is the closing head tag. Once you find that, insert the Analytics HTML code directly before it and save the document by pressing "update file". The Analytics tracking code is now installed.

Note: If there is more than one "</head>" in the header.php document, look for the one that isn't part of a description or note (usually the last one on the document).

Now you can go back to Google Analytics and see if it has confirmed that the code has been properly installed on your website. Once you see that it has, you are done!

Social Media Promotional Techniques: Facebook, Google+, and Twitter

Everyone seems to be very confused about how to use social media to grow a blog, but if you implement the following steps and advice, you'll find that your social media promotion will not only

be very powerful, but almost automated (in other words, will take very little time).

First we're going to talk about how to make each post on your website as "social" as possible. Remember how I told you to make each post you write ABSOLUTELY AMAZING? Well now every time someone reads your post, they're probably going to want to share that amazing post with their friends and family, and not only are we going to encourage that behavior, we're going to make it as easy as possible for them to do so.

At the end of every post I write, I always include the following calls to action:

1. Follow me on any one of my social networks.
2. Share this article on your preferred social network.
3. Leave a comment.
4. Don't forget to join my mailing list.

You'd be surprised how effective this is! My goal is to have every reader perform at least one of those actions. If people enjoyed your article, they'll usually do at least one of those things, and that means you've gained a little more exposure for your blog, and possibly a new lifetime reader.

Note: For some of these calls to action, certain plugins are really helpful. You can watch me install and configure plugins in the video lesson on this page:

http://makemoneyfromhomelionsclub.com/lesson-1-3-how-to-add-social-media-buttons-a-contact-form-google-maps-and-paypal-buttons/

Here is an explanation of how to implement and treat each of the calls to action:

1. Follow me on any social network.

People have different preferences regarding what social network they primarily use. For this reason, I suggest you get your blog on *at least* the big three: Facebook, Google+, and Twitter. If your blog is about something very visual (like photography), then I'd suggest you take a look at also including your blog on Pinterest, Instagram, etc. Any additional network(s) you add is up to you.

Once you've made a profile for your blog for each of the social networks you've selected, it's time to find an elegant way to link to those networks from your blog. Some blogs already have some elegant buttons right in the theme themselves, and if you have one of those themes, all you have to do is activate the buttons (you'll have to figure out how activate the buttons depending on what theme you are using, but it will be somewhere in the theme settings).

If you don't have one of these themes, there are several plugins that will add social media buttons for you. I suggest you look around for a plugin that fits your blog and personal style, but my favorite plugin for adding social media buttons is The Social Links by Digital Leap. With it, your social media buttons will go on your sidebar and will look like this:

Every time you publish a new post, take a few extra minutes to link to that post from each of your social networks (i.e. link to it from your Facebook, Google+, Twitter, etc.). Every person that has followed you on any of those social networks over the years will see your link and (hopefully) check out your new article. In other words, if you are posting one new article per week, that means you will update each of your social networks once a week too.

Hopefully your followers on each of your social networks will re-share your post, giving your article (and blog) more exposure.

2. Share this article on your preferred social network.

With this suggestion, I'm asking the reader not to follow me on a social network, but to share the post on *their* social network. This is how posts go viral: by being shared on social media platforms. And a post going viral is something every blogger should hope for.

For this task, I like to use the plugin Slick Social Share Buttons by Lee Chestnutt. This plugin will add the social share buttons of your choice to posts or pages (or both) on your website.

Note: You can watch me installing and configuring this plugin in the video lesson on this page:

http://makemoneyfromhomelionsclub.com/lesson-1-3-how-to-add-social-media-buttons-a-contact-form-google-maps-and-paypal-buttons/

Once the plugin is installed, the social share buttons will look like this (although you can change where and how it looks in the settings):

Just having the buttons will encourage some people to share the post, but I like to specifically ask the reader to share the post as well.

3. Leave a comment.

Having lots of comments on your posts makes them stronger, so you want to encourage people to comment. This is because with comments more content is being added to your post (as well as diverse opinions), and it acts as a kind of social proof too (if someone sees that your articles generate lots of comments, they'll be more inclined to comment and join the discussion / read more of your blog / follow you on a social network, etc.).

Also, if an active discussion gets started in the comments section, people will keep coming back to your post to follow the discussion.

To assist with getting people to come back to the post to continue the discussion, I like to use the plugin Subscribe to Comments by Mark Jaquith. What this plugin does is it adds a check box under the comment area that allows the person to subscribe to that post. If the person checks off that box, then that person will receive an

email notification every time someone leaves another comment on that blog post.

This is fantastic because it will get readers to return to your blog post to continue the discussion (instead of the blog post and discussion being forgotten about).

4. Don't forget to join my mailing list.

This was already covered in a previous chapter.

Guest Posting and Making Link Requests to Other Webmasters

Note: You can watch me doing the process of link requests by emailing other webmasters in the video lesson on the following page:

http://makemoneyfromhomelionsclub.com/lesson-5-2-how-to-build-links-by-submitting-articles-and-link-requests/

Guest posting is the practice of writing a post for another blog, and the webmaster of that blog will allow a link or two within the article to your blog. They get some free content for their blog and you get a link or two for your blog: it's a win-win. This method is done by actually emailing other webmasters and asking for a link directly from their website to your website.

Not only will the guest post provide you with some direct traffic from the link (and hopefully gain you some new loyal readers), but your blog will receive a slight Seach Engine Optimization (SEO) boost that will make the website a bit stronger and help it rank better in search engines.

The reason this method is powerful is because you will be asking webmasters for links from other websites to your website that are in *your same category*. In other words, if I was looking for links for

my Cement and Concrete Construction Guide website, I'd be emailing other webmasters that have websites related to construction. If one of those websites were to link to mine, that would be one of the most powerful links I could hope for (because it is coming from a genuine website instead of an article directory AND it is related to my category / niche).

To ask for links from other webmasters is actually a fairly simple process; the difficult part is getting another webmaster to actually agree to it (since most of them simply won't reply to your request or just refuse to give you a link from their website).

In some cases, the webmaster will agree to give you a link if you will give them a link from one of your websites in return (a trade). In these cases I usually oblige, since I have nothing to lose by linking to another website from one of mine. In fact, linking to other websites that you like is a practice that Google encourages (it is how the Internet works, after all!).

A simple way to find websites related to your website that may link to you is by doing a Google search for your website topic. Once you do your search, just send out an email to each and every website that has some kind of contact information. The email should be something along these lines:

Subject: Interested in a Link Exchange from www.YOURWEBSITE.com

Message: Dear webmaster,

I am the owner of www.YOURWEBSITE.com and I really like your website. I also have a website that offers great information on "topic." If you would like to exchange links (through guest posting or otherwise), I would be happy to do so. Please let me know if this is something you would be interested in.

The link information is:

Anchor Text: Website Title
URL: www.YOURWEBSITE.com

Thanks,

Mike

Note: This is a numbers game. You may email 50 different website owners, get a reply from only 10, and get an actual link from just five. Just email as many webmasters as you can, asking for links. These links from other related websites are the BEST kinds of links that you can get (to get some direct traffic from other websites in your niche as well as boost your website in the search engine results).

Note: As I'm sure you are realizing, building this passive income website portfolio takes a lot of writing. If you want to outsource your writing, there are resources for doing that on my resources page:
http://makemoneyfromhomelionsclub.com/resources/ **(under "Content Creation"). Some of these services will even submit your articles for you with the specific anchor text you choose. Even if you aren't financially ready to start outsourcing the writing, I would recommend everyone eventually do it at some point. That is the way to eventually grow this business exponentially and on auto-pilot while freeing up your time.**

How to Build Backlinks using HubPages, Free Online Blogs, Forum Commenting, and Blog Commenting

Now we're going to discuss a few other methods for building backlinks to your websites (for direct traffic, plus a Search Engine Optimization (SEO) boost).

Note: You can watch how I submit articles to HubPages, build backlinks using free online blogs, and do proper forum / blog commenting on the video lesson on the following page:

http://makemoneyfromhomelionsclub.com/lesson-5-3-how-to-build-links-using-hubpages-free-online-blogs-forum-commenting-and-blog-commenting/

HubPages

Note: You can sign up for a HubPages account by clicking here:

http://makemoneyfromhomelionsclub.com/hubpages

You can also sign up here:

http://makemoneyfromhomelionsclub.com/resources/ **(under "Link Building Tools").**

HubPages is a unique online article directory because of one special detail: they allow you to monetize the articles you submit with Google Adsense and Amazon Associates (and they split the revenue made from the articles with you). Therefore you are getting the best of both worlds: great backlinks to your websites AND making money off of those articles that you submitted.

This is great because HubPages is a very powerful website and will provide your websites with some great links, but you also have the potential to make money off those articles you submitted as well!

This is a better deal than many other article directories that simply take ALL the earnings your article makes.

There are many people who make a living solely from income generated from their HubPages account (they just submit hundreds and hundreds of articles). I, however, wouldn't recommend doing that: building your entire business on someone else's website

doesn't strike me as the wisest or most secure choice. I'd rather build a business on websites that I own and always have full control.

Even so, HubPages is a great place to gain some experience, gain some back links to your main website(s), and make some money while you're doing it!

When submitting articles to HubPages I would make the following recommendations:

- Make the articles 500-1000 words each.
- Don't forget to register your Google Adsense and Amazon Associates information so you can make money from the articles you submit.
- Include the following capsules (at the very least) to ensure you have a high quality hub: text capsule, Amazon capsule, photos capsule, links capsule, and comments capsule.
- Be sure to include at least two links to your main websites, at least one link to an authority website (like Wikipedia, New York Times, etc.) and the rest of the links should be to products on Amazon with your affiliate information.

Free Online Blogs

Another great resource for powerful backlinks are free online blogs, and the two most powerful ones are Blogspot and Blogger. You can create your own miniblogs on these websites, and the miniblogs will be pretty strong because they will be hosted directly on blogspot.com and blogger.com (which are very powerful websites). Then you can use these miniblogs to link directly to your main websites.

Here is how I would suggest constructing your miniblogs for your websites:

- Make the miniblog at least five posts total with 500-1000 words each.

- Monetize these miniblogs with Google Adsense or Amazon Associates or both (why not, right?).
- Be sure to include at least two links to your main websites, at least one link to an authority website (like Wikipedia, New York Times, etc.) and the rest of the links should be to products on Amazon with your affiliate information.
- Include photos for each post (with targeted keywords in title) and at least one related YouTube video somewhere on the blog.

These miniblogs will generate some traffic and money on their own and provide some very powerful links to your main websites. I would recommend creating a Blogspot miniblog and a Blogger miniblog for each one of your websites.

Blog and Forum Commenting

Commenting on blogs or within forums is another great way to get some backlinks and strengthen your website(s). Even though these backlinks are somewhat weak, they are another source of backlinks and every little bit helps! In addition to providing your website with some backlinks, the main reason behind these comments is direct traffic from other readers who like your comments and end up visiting your website.

Also remember that some of the readers may be webmasters, and if you develop a relationship with them by creating a dialog through commenting, they may end up linking to your website from theirs (that is the best outcome you could hope for from these efforts!). This is the type of mentality you have to have when promoting your blog(s) when doing blog and forum commenting.

When commenting on forums or on blog posts, don't forget these guidelines:

- Sign every comment with your name and website URL.
- Try to make each comment something that ADDS to the conversation.

- Try to develop a relationship with other webmasters, so that you can later request links to your website or request to submit guest posts to their website (with a link pointing back to your website).
- Be honest and genuine in your forum commenting. If you're jumping from forum to forum simply trying to pump out as many comments as possible without adding anything to the conversation, it's not going to be effective for you (a lot of spammers do this sort of thing and people hate it).

Do this kind of promotion through commenting for your blog(s) to get some direct traffic and develop a relationship with other webmasters that could end up giving you links to your websites.

Note: Forum commenting is something that can also be outsourced. If you want to outsource your forum commenting, there are resources for doing that on my resources page: http://makemoneyfromhomelionsclub.com/resources/ **(under "Outsourcing").**

Advanced Link Building Using PostRunner

Another extremely powerful link building tool I am going to recommend is PostRunner.

Note: You can watch how I use PostRunner on the video lesson on the following page:

http://makemoneyfromhomelionsclub.com/lesson-5-5-advanced-link-building-using-postrunner/

If you are interested in joining PostRunner, you can join at a discounted rate by clicking here:

http://makemoneyfromhomelionsclub.com/postrunner

You can also join at a discounted rate on this page:

http://makemoneyfromhomelionsclub.com/resources/ **(it is listed under "Link Building Tools").**

PostRunner is a tool where you can submit guest posts for backlinks through a main user interface, and that article will be posted on any website of your choice within the system (there are thousands of websites within the system to choose from, across all categories). It is essentially a system for "guest posting", except you don't have to email the webmaster to guest post on their website – they are already in PostRunner because they want to receive guest posts!

The websites you can submit to are all owned by individual PostRunner users (instead of one big entity), so it makes the backlinks you get perfectly safe to use directly on your main websites and extremely powerful overall. The websites are all rated with several different metrics (PageRank, user score, etc.) and each have their article requirements listed right within the system, so you can select the websites you'd like to post on and write your articles accordingly.

These articles that you post will give your website exposure to a new audience and the links will help with your search engine rankings.

In addition to the wide range of websites you can submit your articles to, you can also opt to have your own blog(s) within the system (as long as they are made with WordPress). With your websites within the system, you can accept guest posts from other bloggers who also use PostRunner. In other words, you are also on the other side of the process (an article directory) – receiving articles instead of only submitting them.

I would recommend you put your blog(s) in the PostRunner system so you can start receiving free content and really take advantage of this tool. As you know, more posts equals more content which equals more traffic which equals more money. It's free content on your website in exchange for a backlink to the blogger who

submitted the article. It's a win-win and that is why I like this tool so much.

In addition to including all your blogs in PostRunner for the free content your websites will receive, I'd recommend submitting at least one article to each related blog that you can within PostRunner, for each blog that you own. You will be able to get several backlinks from several different websites, but all within related categories to your own websites. This is what makes this tool so powerful, and these links will strengthen your blogs even more.

Note: As I'm sure you are realizing, building this passive income website portfolio takes a lot of writing. If you want to outsource your writing, there are resources for doing that on my resources page: http://makemoneyfromhomelionsclub.com/resources/ **(under "Content Creation"). Some of these services will even submit your articles for you with the specific anchor text you choose. Even if you aren't financially ready to start outsourcing the writing, I would recommend everyone eventually do it at some point. That is the way to eventually grow this business exponentially and on auto-pilot while freeing up your time.**

A Quick Note on YouTube

YouTube is the second biggest search engine in the world (after Google).

The amount of content being uploaded on YouTube is staggering - 48 hours worth of footage per minute. Their website gets over three BILLION hits per day. If you don't have a YouTube presence, you are potentially missing out on huge amounts of direct traffic (not to mention the indirect SEO benefits of having a few links from YouTube pointing back to your blog!).

Regardless of what type of industry your blog is in or the type of

blog that it is, making a decent high-quality video is not hard, and the process of uploading it onto YouTube is extremely simple.

You should **at least** make one video describing who you are and what your blog can offer. There is no downside to putting yourself on the second largest search engine in the world!

And one final tip: when you make your description for the video on YouTube, make sure the very first thing you write down is your website URL (like I have in all of mine) - the display of the description on YouTube is tiny so you want to make sure the link to your website is the very first thing on there.

Final Thoughts on Blog Promotion and Link Building

In this chapter we have covered some of the most effective promotional and link building methods that exist, and they are also some of the safest and most conservative (in other words, they don't risk a penalization from Google). They are all "white hat" techniques, and maybe approaching "gray hat" at the most – never "black hat."

These methods include social media promotion, article submissions, link exchanges, guest posts, blog and forum commenting, building links from HubPages, PostRunner, and our own miniblogs.

Between all these methods, you have everything you need to get your blog lots and lots of traffic. These types of link building techniques are all manual (not automated), which makes them the most tedious to build, but it also makes them the safest, the most powerful, and the best for the overall growth and longevity of your blog(s). When you are not writing posts for your blog(s), your time should be spent promoting your blog(s) and making them stronger over time.

As you progress in your online career, you're going to realize there are thousands of link building tools being sold that promise things like "it is completely safe", "it is completely automated", "it will explode your online business with the click of a button", etc. Be wary of all these kinds of products! More than likely the product doesn't do what it promises, and could even jeopardize your business in the long run. These products usually only exist to make the owner money from sales of that product.

Stick to the promotional techniques described above (even though they are the most tedious), and you will be successful in the long run.

Remember: if you do the work that others are unwilling to do, you will get the results that others will never achieve.

FINAL THOUGHTS ON THIS BUSINESS

Everything taught in this book essentially comes down to one main goal: driving free traffic to your blog(s) and converting that traffic into lifelong readers.

Like so many things in life, making money online is a numbers game. More blog posts = more traffic = more money. THAT is the foundation of making money online.

Also remember that money inevitably goes toward quality products. Make your blog(s) the best you possibly can and it will pay off in the long run. If you bring value to your readers, they will reciprocate: it could be through links, shares, comments, recommending your blog to their friends / family, or buying your product(s).

Don't be afraid to take the lessons in this book and then experiment and explore with other ideas. Making MASSIVE amounts of online income isn't a dream, but it does take patience, dedication, and persistence!

Please spread the word about my book and my websites to your friends and family! Learning these skills (even if it's *just* how to build a WordPress website) is extremely empowering, and I'd love to encourage everyone to try their hand at entrepreneurship and hopefully inspire them to create things beyond what this book teaches!

Thank you for reading, and remember: if you do the work that others are unwilling to do, you will get the results that others will never achieve.

BONUS CHAPTER: HOW TO DO YOUR OWN BOOKKEEPING AND ACCOUNTING

I decided to come back and add this small chapter after the release of the book because it is something I frequently get emailed about (that's why it is here at the end haha).

A simple reality about running your own business is that you have to take care of your bookkeeping and accounting work (to be prepared for tax season). It turns out this is a lot easier to do than I had ever imagined, and doing this work actually helps you understand your own business better.

FreshBooks is the new gold standard for small business accounting software. QuickBooks (the old standard) is getting dumped across America for this much more intuitive and user-friendly product. I used to be terrified of anything related to the words "accounting", "bookkeeping", and "taxes", mostly because I didn't understand anything about that world. This software was recommended by my CPA to keep my finances organized for my business. With this software you'll end up realizing that maintaining your own bookkeeping / accounting is quite simple – the program walks you through how to do it.

If you go to my resources page, you'll find a link under "Bookkeeping and Accounting" where you can try FreshBooks free for 30 days: http://makemoneyfromhomelionsclub.com/resources

I hope you have enjoyed my book! If so, please leave a positive review on Amazon.com and help spread the word!

This ebook was brought to you by http://makemoneyfromhomelionsclub.com.

If you are interested in entrepreneurship, making passive income online, and other ways to make money outside of a standard job, be sure to visit http://makemoneyfromhomelionsclub.com!

In the first video lesson you are taught the entire process of how http://mikeomarphotography.com was made from beginning to end, without the need of any coding knowledge, in under one hour!

With the lessons taught there, you will be able to make yourself a professional website with any kind of look that you want.

There are also lessons on Search Engine Optimization (SEO), social media promotion, making mailing lists, selling ebooks and other digital products, developing passive income online, and more. There are also lessons on how to make money with Google, Amazon, and ClickBank (all passive!).

Note: All of the links within this book can be found easily from my main website:

http://makemoneyfromhomelionsclub.com

I love connecting with my readers and something I like to do is personally help them with their online financial goals.

I'd be happy to help you find success in any way that I can.

Please feel free to send me an email telling me who you are, why you are interested in making money online, what your online income goals are, and how you found out about my online school. You can email me via the "contact" page of the LIONS CLUB website.

You can find all of my ebooks at
http://makemoneyfromhomelionsclub.com/amazon

Mike Omar

My books:

HOW TO MAKE A WEBSITE OR BLOG: with WordPress WITHOUT Coding, on your own domain, all in under 2 hours.
http://makemoneyfromhomelionsclub.com/ebook1

HOW TO MAKE MONEY ONLINE: Learn how to make money from home with my step-by-step plan to build a $5000 per month passive income website portfolio (based on building 10 websites that make at least $500 per month each).
http://makemoneyfromhomelionsclub.com/ebook

HOW TO START A BLOG THAT PEOPLE WILL READ: How to create a website, write about a topic you love, develop a loyal readership, and make six figures doing it.
http://makemoneyfromhomelionsclub.com/ebookblog

All of the following websites were made using the exact same techniques outlined in this book and video lessons. Any of these websites will be within your ability to create once you complete the lessons:

Make Money from Home LIONS CLUB –
http://makemoneyfromhomelionsclub.com – My main website.

Mike Omar Photography – http://mikeomarphotography.com – My freelancing website where I used to make websites for clients at $500 each (now it simply serves as an example website).

$1,000 / Month Passive Income Website –
http://makemoneyfromhomesamplewebsite.com - This is the structure and layout of a $1,000 / Month Passive Income website monetized with with Google Adsense and Amazon Associates.

Sample Sales Page – http://makemoneyfromhomeinfoproduct.com – A samples sales page template that teaches how to make a website designed to sell a digital product.

How to Become a Ticket Broker –
http://howtobecomeaticketbroker.net - A live example of one of my passive income websites that makes money selling a digital product (an ebook).

High Quality Outsourcing – http://highqualityoutsourcing.com - If you are interested in outsourcing the entire SEO backlinking process through my personal team (to get high rankings for your website(s) for specific keywords in Google and other searches), you can learn about that service here.

A few important things to keep in mind while reading through this book:

Throughout the book you will be referred to video lessons. While everything in the book and video lessons is as up to date as possible (I frequently update this book and the video lessons), the

place to check for the most up-to-date information is in the *video descriptions* (on the same page you watch the videos). This can be the video descriptions on the pages of the LIONS CLUB website, or the video description of wherever you are watching the videos. Be sure to read the video descriptions of each video *before* watching the video itself.

Also, in this book you will find a lot of concepts are repeated. I know some readers will find this somewhat annoying, but several of my readers have told me they really like this because it really reinforces the most important concepts to take away from this book. That is why the book is written this way.

And most important of all: don't forget to sign up for my free weekly LIONS CLUB newsletter. Not only will you get great information with advice on how to make money online and how to build an online business, it is also where I send out updates regarding ranking strategies, new traffic generation techniques, important announcements, etc. Please sign up here:

http://makemoneyfromhomelionsclub.com/newsletter